Routledge Revivals

Catalogue of Chinese Manuscripts in Danish Archives

First published in 1980, *Catalogue of Chinese Manuscripts in Danish Archives* is a descriptive catalogue that gives the date, address, and a summary of the contents for some 500 Chinese manuscripts in three Danish archives: the National Archives, the National Museum, and the Archives of the Great Northern Telegraph Company. The Chinese diplomatic correspondence kept in these archives form important source material for the study of Sino-Danish relations in the nineteenth century. In addition, the contents of the manuscripts shed an interesting light on the way Chinese and foreign diplomacy at the lowest level was conducted during the crucial years of Sino-Western relations. The book contains an introduction and two indexes, one for the names mentioned in the addresses, and one for the subjects and names mentioned in the summaries. The book will appeal to students of history, political science, international relations and diplomacy.

Catalogue of Chinese Manuscripts in Danish Archives

Chinese diplomatic correspondence from the Ch'ing dynasty (1644-1911)

Erik Baark

First published in 1980
by Curzon Press

This edition first published in 2022 by Routledge
4 Park Square, Milton Park, Abingdon, Oxon, OX14 4RN
and by Routledge
605 Third Avenue, New York, NY 10017

Routledge is an imprint of the Taylor & Francis Group, an informa business

© Erik Baark 1979

All rights reserved. No part of this book may be reprinted or reproduced or utilised in any form or by any electronic, mechanical, or other means, now known or hereafter invented, including photocopying and recording, or in any information storage or retrieval system, without permission in writing from the publishers.

Publisher's Note
The publisher has gone to great lengths to ensure the quality of this reprint but points out that some imperfections in the original copies may be apparent.

Disclaimer
The publisher has made every effort to trace copyright holders and welcomes correspondence from those they have been unable to contact.

A Library of Congress record exists under ISBN: 0700701206

ISBN: 978-1-032-32324-4 (hbk)
ISBN: 978-1-003-31467-7 (ebk)
ISBN: 978-1-032-32367-1 (pbk)

Book DOI 10.4324/9781003314677

STUDIES ON ASIAN TOPICS NO. 2

CATALOGUE OF CHINESE MANUSCRIPTS IN DANISH ARCHIVES

Chinese diplomatic correspondence from the Ch'ing dynasty (1644–1911)

ERIK BAARK

CURZON PRESS

SCANDINAVIAN INSTITUTE OF ASIAN STUDIES
Kejsergade 2, DK-1155 Copenhagen K

First published 1980

Curzon Press Ltd : London and Malmö

© Erik Baark 1979

ISBN 0 7007 0120 6
ISSN 0142 6208

Printed in Great Britain by
Biddles Ltd, Guildford, Surrey

CONTENTS

Preface	i
Introduction	ii-viii
The Catalogue	ix
Entries 1-522	1-125
The Indexes	127
Index to Names in the Addresses	129-133
Index to Subjects and Names in the Summaries	135-158

To

C. Rise Hansen

PREFACE

The contents of this catalogue are the result of work carried out in periods during the years 1973-1978. The description of the Chinese manuscripts was initiated when C. Rise Hansen was compiling the *Guide to the Sources of the History of North Africa, Asia and Oceania* for Denmark and found Chinese manuscripts in the National Archives which had not been listed or marked in such a way that historians would be able to use the source material they contained. In 1973 I was thus employed as a student assistant to make a list of a limited number of Chinese manuscripts in the Consular Archives of Shanghai and Foochow. In 1974-1975 new manuscripts were found in other files and in 1976 I finally made a list, more or less in a form similar to the present catalogue, including 285 documents. I presented this list as an appendix to my thesis on Sino-Danish diplomatic relations during the Ch'ing dynasty, and after I had graduated in Sinology from the University of Copenhagen, I wanted to publish the material which I had been working with for over four years. A grant from the Carlsberg Foundation made it possible to complete the catalogue, including some 200 manuscripts which had been left out in my previous list. In addition, I was able to prepare the Introduction, the Indexes and finally the manuscript for the catalogue in its present form.

At times, one cannot help wondering whether this kind of research has any purpose; but during the period I was working on this catalogue, the enthusiasm of Overarkivar C. Rise Hansen always helped to keep the fire burning.

I am also grateful to Kresten Nielsen for his suggestion to prepare the indexes on a computer, a project which was carried through with the help from Jørgen Døssing and the support from the Scandinavian Institute of Asian Studies. Donald B. Wagner has made great efforts to make my amateurish English become intelligible.

Finally, the Carlsberg Foundation has also supported the publication of this volume, and has thus been instrumental in ensuring the successful completion of this project.

Copenhagen, May 1979

Erik Baark

INTRODUCTION

The present catalogue covers Chinese manuscripts and xylographs dating from the Ch'ing dynasty (1644-1911) which have been kept by the following archives in Copenhagen:

The National Archives.
Rigsarkivet,
Rigsdagsgården 9,
1218 Copenhagen K.

The National Museum. The Ethnographical Department.
Nationalmuseet, Etnografisk Samling,
Prinsens Palais,
Frederiksholms Kanal 12,
1220 Copenhagen K.

The Archives of the Great Northern Telegraph Company.
Det Store Nordiske Telegraf-selskab A/S,
Kongens Nytorv 26-28,
1050 Copenhagen K.

  The Royal Library in Copenhagen has a collection of Chinese manuscripts and xylographs which has not been included in this catalogue for two reasons. First, the collection contains very few diplomatic documents as such. Second, the Royal Library intends to compile a thorough catalogue including all Chinese manuscripts in the years to come.
  In the following sections I shall try to describe the collections that form the main background of this catalogue.

The National Archives

In the National Archives the following collections are represented in the catalogue*:

1. Udenrigsministeriets Arkiv (The Archives of the Ministry of Foreign Affairs):
    Gesandtskabsarkiver. Peking. (Legation Archives, Peking).
    Konsulatsarkiver. (Consulate Archives): Chefoo, Foochow Foo, Shanghai, Swatow.
    Kommercekollegiets Arkiv. Samlede Sager. (Department of Trade and Consulates. Selected Files).
    Traktater. Kina. (Treaties. China).
2. Privaltarkiver (Private Archives):
    Admiral Steen Andersen Bille's (†1883) Arkiv.
3. Ostindisk og Asiatisk Kompagni's Arkiv. (Archives of the Royal Danish Asiatic Company).

There are only a few Chinese manuscripts in the Legation Archives, the Private Archives and the archives of the Royal Danish Asiatic Company. The main part of the material treated in this catalogue has been found in the Consulate Archives, in particular in the Consulate Archives from Shanghai and Foochow. These two archives deserve to be analysed and described in a longer paper, but here I have included a short description which I hope will serve as an introduction to the source-material they contain.

The Consulate Archives from Shanghai include the following material:

    Letter Books 1893-1919. (8 vols.)
    Correspondence etc. 1842-1894. (9 bundles)
    In-letters 1894-1904. (3 bundles)
    Various Correspondence 1896-1904. (2 bundles)
    Correspondence etc. 1904-1925. (92 bundles)

The correspondence is arranged according to the affairs of the Consulate in a chronological sequence.

* For further reference, see C. Rise Hansen: *"Guide to the Sources of the History of North Africa, Asia and Oceania. Denmark."* Published under the Auspices of the UNESCO and of the International Council on Archives. To be published in 1979-80 by Verlag Dokumentation in München.

For the correspondence there exist the following Journals compiled by the Consuls:

1894-96 Journal for in- and out-letters (with alphabetical register).
1897-1904 Journal for out-letters (with alphabetical register).
1905-08 Journal for out-letters.
1904-08 Journal (Alphabetical register for each year).
1908-1924 Journal (Alphabetical register).

After 1925 a new system for the journalizing of the archives of the diplomatic representatives of Denmark was introduced by the Ministry of Foreign Affairs, whereby the archives of the Danish Consulate at Shanghai were arranged according to a system corresponding closely to that of the Ministry of Foreign Affairs. At present there are 227 bundles with correspondence from the time after 1925. For this material there are also 23 Journals compiled by the Consuls. Unfortunately all of this well-arranged historical source material is covered by the secrecy-clause maintained by the Ministry of Foreign Affairs, a clause which makes all correspondence of private character inaccessible for a period of 50 years. The Ministry of Foreign Affairs can, however, issue a special permit for a historian to use this valuable material.

The consulate archives were transferred to Denmark from the Consulate-General in Shanghai in 1946. Characteristically the archives seem to have been found in dusty boxes during a general clean-up action in the Consulate-General. After they had been transferred to the Ministry of Foreign Affairs in Denmark, they were almost immediately handed over to the National Archives, where they were re-packed in the bundle-wrappings used by the National Archives.

The consular archives from Shanghai which date from the years before 1904 have either not been maintained properly by the Danish consuls or have fallen into a mess in a later period. The most convincing suggestion is that they have not been kept on a continued basis by different consuls. First, a glance through the catalogue will show that the amount of Chinese correspondence which has been kept in the archives varies according to the particular consul in office at that moment. For example, during the years 1859-1866 the consuls at Shanghai, who were agents of the British firm Jardine, Matheson and Co., have kept the records quite conscientiously, while the period 1866-1888 shows a complete lack of Chinese correspondence from Shanghai.

Only after the arrival of Peter Theodor Raaschou to the post as Consul-General of Denmark at Shanghai in 1904, do the records seem to have been kept in an orderly way. Likewise, the Russian consuls at Fuchou have been more conscientious with regard to the Chinese correspondence than most of the consuls who were employed by the Danish government in the Chinese cities.

Second, there is some confusion as to where the Chinese correspondence should be placed. One particular bundle in the Consulate Archives of Shanghai (2035 Konsulatsarkiver. Shanghai. Korrespondancesager m.v. 1842-94: *Pakke 9*) contains only Chinese letters and has been marked "various Chinese letters with unidentifiable dates". It is uncertain whether the Chinese correspondence has been plucked out from ordinary correspondence at the consulate in Shanghai or during the re-packing at the National Archives. I personally think that it is quite plausible that this was done at the consulate in Shanghai as the isolation of the Chinese letters was never carried out systematically and because it is contrary to the ethics of professional archivists to re-shuffle correspondence of any sort. Maybe the isolation of Chinese letters was an attempt by a well-meaning consul to avoid sending to Denmark something which might never be of interest on account of the language barrier.

Another puzzle in the Consulate Archives from Shanghai is the presence of correspondence from what should properly be identified as the Consulate Archives of Fuchou. The extensive Chinese correspondence concerning the telegraphline which the Great Northern Telegraph Company wanted to build between Fuchou and Amoy in 1874-1877 seems to have slipped into the correspondence from Shanghai. A possible explanation is that the Danish Consul in Shanghai received copies of the correspondence addressed to the Danish Consulate in Fuchou, at the time managed by the Consul of the United States of America, M.M. DeLano. Some of the letters, however, appear to be originals and there seems to be no reason why the Danish Consul at Shanghai should receive originals as well as copies of the correspondence. The only explanation left is that the archives of the two consulates were mixed by a mistake before they were transferred to Denmark.

The examples mentioned above show that the Chinese correspondence in the National Archives which date from the Ch'ing dynasty is not easily identifiable and located in a confusing manner; this catalogue is intended to be a help for those interested in the Chinese sources placed in this archive.

The National Museum

The Ethnographical Department of the National Museum has a collection of Chinese manuscripts which is made up largely on the basis of gifts from the Royal Danish Asiatic Company and the Danish Ministry of Foreign Affairs. The documents in the collection date from a period earlier than 1860 and therefore supplement the collection at the National Archives, where all Chinese correspondence seems to have been placed after 1860. The documents at the National Museum are thus the basic, although fragmentary, Chinese source material in Denmark for the study of early Sino-Danish diplomatic relationship.

The Archives of the Great Northern Telegraph Company

One of the most important events in the Sino-Danish diplomatic relationship during the Ch'ing dynasty was undoubtedly the establishment of telegraphs in China by the Great Northern Telegraph Company. The National Archives have a large number of documents that throw some light on the role of the Great Northern Telegraph Company in the introduction of telegraphs to China. In addition to this, the Directors of the Great Northern Telegraph Company have kindly permitted me to see some selected key documents from the files of the company's archives. These I have included in the catalogue.

The Arrangement of the Manuscripts in the Catalogue

I have decided to arrange the entries in the catalogue according to a chronological sequence. I have done this for three reasons. First, the manuscripts included have been found in different files where the arrangement according to files did not to my mind render any sensible approach to the subjects mentioned in the documents. Second, the arrangement of the Chinese manuscripts in the files have neither been done in a strictly subject-orientated nor chronological order. Third, the subjects covered by the entries in the catalogue are indeed manifold, partly because I decided at an early date to make this catalogue a catch-all affair with reference to the Chinese manuscripts, regardless of the trivialities which it has been necessary to include. All in all, I found the chronological arrangement the most practical for my own purposes, and to make the catalogue practical for others, I have worked out an index of the subjects and the names which are mentioned in the summaries and an index of the names mentioned in the addresses.

Identification of Names

One of the major problems confronting me during the preparation of the catalogue was the identification of names, Chinese as well as European.

Sometimes the Chinese officials are mentioned by surname only and I have used as many sources as possible to identify their personal names. Likewise, the names of Europeans are transcribed into Chinese characters in the documents and though the correspondence in western languages often gives definite clues to the identifications, many names were left unidentified.

In addition, the addresses which are stated in the entries are not always mentioned on the documents but have been based on my personal knowledge of the circumstances in which the document in question was made. As a general rule, the names and titles of the Chinese officials are indicated on official communications, while only the names are written on the letters. In this connection, I have to excuse one of the shortcomings, from a sinological point of view, of this catalogue namely the absence of Chinese characters in the summaries and in the indexes.

Translations of Titles etc.

For the translations of the official Chinese titles I have followed H.S. Brunnert and V.V. Hagelstrom: *Present Day Political Organization of China*. (Shanghai 1912). Therefore the term Intendant has been used instead of the term Taotai, which is more widely used in sinological circles.

I have used the study by J.K. Fairbank and S.Y. Teng: *Ch'ing Administration: Three Studies*. (Cambridge, Mass. 1960) for the translations of the Chinese terms for official correspondence. For example, *chao-hui* has been translated as "communication".

Identification of Dates

The identification of dates was probably the most difficult work I had to do during the preparation of this catalogue. I have had to establish some sort of a date for each document as the catalogue was arranged according to the dates of the entries.

Again, when the proper information was lacking on the Chinese manuscript, I have had to determine the dates from my knowledge of the circumstances in which a document may have been produced. I suspect, however, that the dates for some of the 522 entries might still be wrong, thus placing them out of their proper context, but the indexes should help the reader to locate all material relevant to any particular case. In any case, I have written the reconstructed parts of the dates in a parenthesis, an indication of the fact that these parts should be read with due reservations.

THE CATALOGUE

The catalogue has been arranged in a chronological sequence: therefore the manuscripts have been provided with a regular reference to the actual signature for its location in the respective archives.

Each item has been described, as far as it has been possible to reconstruct the facts, with the following information:

1. The date.
   This has been stated in the Julian calendar as well as the ordinary Chinese date, which reads: reign title, year of reign, month, day.
2. The sender.
   Usually Chinese officials. In general, the document will mention either the title and the surname of the Chinese official or his name in full. In the entry, the title has been abbreviated and sometimes the name or the title or both are reconstructed from evidence found in the document.
3. The receiver.
   Usually foreign consuls. They are only mentioned in the documents by the Chinese character which is the initial character in the transcription of their names. I have derived the actual names from other sources available.
4. Summary of the contents of the manuscripts.
   The excerpt tries to summarize the most important information contained in the manuscripts. I have indicated the type of diplomatic document used, e.g. a communication or a letter. Unfortunately I have not found time to include information on the size of the manuscripts, the type of paper used, etc.
5. Reference for the document.
   The signature after the summary indicates (in Danish) the location of the document in the archives; it is my hope that the signature is sufficient for an easy identification of the document. The signatures beginning with a code number refers to the archives in the National Archives, e.g.:
   = 2035 Konsulatsarkiver. Shanghai . . .
   = Nationalmuseet signifies that the document is located in the National Museum, while
   = Store Nordiske Arkiv signifies the archives of the Great Northern Telegraph Company.

1.

Date: (19 December 1736), - Ch'ien-lung, 1, 11, 18.
From: O-Mi-Ta, Governor-general of Kwangtung and
Kwangsi + Yang Yung-pin, Governor of Kwangtung, Canton.
Proclamation stating that an Imperial Edict has been
received stating that according to the ancient procedure,
it is illegal that the foreign ships maintain their guns
onboard when they sail up to Canton. The procedure
followed recently, to levy an extra tax instead of the
unloading of the guns, is hereby abolished.
= Nationalmuseet.

2.

Date: (16 July 1835) - Tao-kuang 15, 6, 21.
Bill for the sum of 9600 taels plus 18 months interest
of 1460 taels, paid in Canton by a Captain from the
"Huang-ch'i" company, i.e. the Danish "Asiatisk
Kompagni".
= Ostindisk og Asiatisk Kompagni: A. 1. Nr. 206 c.
Diverse Dokumenter 1830-1845.

3.

Date: (3 July 1845) - Tao-kuang 25, 5, 29.
From: Ch'i-ying, Governor-general of Kwangtung and
Kwangsi + Huang, Governor of Kwangtung, Canton.
To: Peter Hansen, Governor of Trankebar, Danish Envoy
to China.
Instructions acknowledging a report from the Danish
Envoy to China, Peter Hansen, stating that the Envoy has
recently arrived in Canton to examine the newly-
established regulations and to negotiate with the Chinese
authorities concerning trade between the two countries.
Ch'i-ying states that because the Chinese Emperor will
treat all foreign nations with equal favour and because
the Danes for some time have traded peacefully in Canton,
the Chinese authorities will approve further negotiations
on establishment of consulates in China and trade
regulations. Copies of the commercial regulations and
duty tariffs are hereby forwarded.
= Nationalmuseet.

4.

Date: (12 October 1847) - (Tao-kuang 27), 9, 9.
From: D.B. Robertson, Consul of Great Britain, Shanghai.
To: Lin Kuei, Military Intendant, Shanghai.
Copy of letter announcing that the Danish Consul-general
to Manila on Lüzon island, Ferdinand Wolff, has arrived
in Shanghai. He requests an audience with the Military
Intendant of Shanghai, Lin Kuei.
= Nationalmuseet, Ba 90 a.

5.

Date: (12 October 1847) - (Tao-kuang 27), 9, 9.
From: Lin Kuei, Military Intendant, Shanghai.
To: D.B. Robertson, Consul of Great Britain, Shanghai.
Copy of letter stating that a meeting can be arranged between the Military Intendant of Shanghai, Lin Kuei, and the Danish Consul-general to Manila, Ferdinand Wolff, on the 19th inst., at two o'clock.
= Nationalmuseet, Ba 90 b.

6.

Date: (23 October 1847) - (Tao-kuang 27), 9, 15.
From: D.B. Robertson, Consul of Great Britain, Shanghai.
To: Lin Kuei, Military Intendant, Shanghai.
Copy of a letter stating that the Intendant is invited to visit the British Consulate on the 24th inst. in connection with the visit of the Danish Consul-general to Manila, Ferdinand Wolff.
= Nationalmuseet, Ba 90 c.

7.

Date: 22 August 1851.
From: Wu Hsü, Acting Military Intendant, Shanghai.
To: D.B. Robertson, Consul of Great Britain, Shanghai.
Copy of a communication stating that on account of the recent negotiations the Intendant hereby forwards a copy of the New Regulations for the Customs. The Consul is requested to let his subjects and Consuls from other countries be informed about these new regulations.
= Kommercekollegiet, Samlede Sager til Konsulatsjournal, Nr. 515.

8.

Date: (29 November 1857) - Hsien-feng 7, 10, 14.
From: Hsüeh Huan, Military Intendant, Shanghai.
To: Alexander Percival, Consul of Denmark, Shanghai.
Communication stating that it is strictly prohibited by the Chinese laws to sail Chinese emigrants to foreign countries.
= 2035 Konsulatsarkiver. Shanghai. Korrespondancesager m.v. 1842-94: Pakke 9, nr. 1.

9.

Date: (19 December 1857) - Hsien-feng 7, 11, 4.
From: Hsüeh Huan, Military Intendant, Shanghai.
To: Alexander Percival, Consul of Denmark, Shanghai.
Letter notifying that the Magistrate's Office is closed on the day of the Winter Solstice, the 22nd of December.
= 2035 Konsulatsarkiver. Shanghai. Korrespondancesager m.v. 1842-94: Pakke 9, nr. 19.

10.

Date: (31 January 1858) - Hsien-feng 7, 12, 17.
From: Hsüeh Huan, Military Intendant, Shanghai.
To: Alexander Percival, Consul of Denmark, Shanghai.
Communication acknowledging the appointment of the
Vice-Consul of the United States of America.
= 2035 Konsulatsarkiver. Shanghai. Korrespondancesager
m.v. 1842-94: Pakke 9, nr. 5.

11.

Date: (23 January 1859) - Hsien-feng 8, 12, 20.
From: Wu Hsü, Intendant, Shanghai.
To: James Whittall, Consul of Denmark, Shanghai.
Communication notifying the appointment of Wu Hsü as
Inspector of Customs in Kiangsu.
= 2035 Konsulatsarkiver. Shanghai. Korrespondancesager
m.v. 1842-94: Pakke 9, nr. 27.

12.

Date: (4 February 1859) - Hsien-feng 9, 1, 2.
From: Wu Hsü, Intendant, Shanghai.
To: James Whittall, Consul of Denmark, Shanghai.
Communication notifying that on the 6th of February
Wu Hsü is to travel to Nanking on official business.
= 2035 Konsulatsarkiver. Shanghai. Korrespondancesager
m.v. 1842-94: Pakke 9, nr. 22.

13.

Date: (18 February 1859) - Hsien-feng 9, 1, 16.
From: Wu Hsü, Intendant, Shanghai.
To: James Whittall, Consul of Denmark, Shanghai.
Communication stating that on the 16th February Wu Hsü
has returned from a trip to Nanking on official business.
= 2035 Konsulatsarkiver. Shanghai. Korrespondancesager
m.v. 1842-94: Pakke 9, nr. 17.

14.

Date: (2 July 1859) - Hsien-feng 9, 6, 3.
From: Wu Hsü, Intendant, Shanghai.
To: James Whittall, Consul of Denmark, Shanghai.
Communication acknowledging the appointment of the
Acting Consul of France. The Consul, C. de Montiguy,
is to travel to Canton.
= 2035 Konsulatsarkiver. Shanghai. Korrespondancesager
m.v. 1842-94: Pakke 9, nr. 59.

15.

Date: (27 July 1859) - Hsien-feng 9, 6, 28.
From: Wu Hsü, Intendant, Shanghai.
To: James Whittall, Consul of Denmark, Shanghai.
Communication acknowledging the appointment of the Acting Consul of Great Britain, T.T. Meadows. The previous Consul, D.B. Robertson, has retired.
= 2035 Konsulatsarkiver. Shanghai. Korrespondancesager m.v. 1842-94: Pakke 9, nr. 12.

16.

Date: (14 August 1859) - Hsien-feng, 9, 7, 16.
From: Wu Hsü, Intendant, Shanghai.
To: James Whittall, Consul of Denmark, Shanghai.
Communication acknowledging the appointment of the Consul of Hamburg. The previous Consul, William Hogg, has retired.
= 2035 Konsulatsarkiver. Shanghai. Korrespondancesager m.v. 1842-94: Pakke 9, nr. 25.

17.

Date: (29 October 1859) - Hsien-feng 9, 10, 4.
From: Wu Hsü, Intendant, Shanghai.
To: James Whittall, Consul of Denmark, Shanghai.
Communication acknowledging the appointment of the Consul of Oldenburg, W. Probst, to act as the Consul of Hanover.
= 2035 Konsulatsarkiver. Shanghai. Korrespondancesager m.v. 1842-94: Pakke 9, nr. 7.

18.

Date: (30 October 1859) - Hsien-feng 9, 10, 5.
From: Wu Hsü, Intendant, Shanghai.
To: James Whittall, Consul of Denmark, Shanghai.
Communication stating that on the 31st of October Wu Hsü is to travel to K'un-shan on official business.
= 2035 Konsulatsarkiver. Shanghai. Korrespondancesager m.v. 1842-94: Pakke 9, nr. 6.

19.

Date: 1 March 1860 - Hsien-feng 10, 2, 9.
From: Wu Hsü, Intendant, Shanghai.
To: James Whittall, Consul of Denmark, Shanghai.
Communication in reply acknowledging the appointment of James Whittall as Consul of Denmark at Shanghai.
= 2035 Konsulatsarkiver. Shanghai. Korrespondancesager m.v. 1842-94: Pakke 1, nr. 1.

20.

Date: (12 March 1860) - Hsien-feng 10, 2, 20.
From: Wu Hsü, Intendant, Shanghai.
To: James Whittall, Consul of Denmark, Shanghai.
Communication acknowledging the appointment of the
Consul of Hamburg, R. Heinsen, who assumes the
responsibility of the Consulate, which previously was
under the jurisdiction of the Consul of Bremen.
= 2035 Konsulatsarkiver. Shanghai. Korrespondancesager
m.v. 1842-94: Pakke 9, nr. 26.

21.

Date: (10 June 1860) - Hsien-feng 10, 4, 21.
From: Wu Hsü, Intendant, Shanghai.
To: James Whittall, Consul of Denmark, Shanghai.
Communication acknowledging the appointment of the
Consul of Russia. Furthermore, Wu Hsü states that he
has not received any instructions from the authorities
concerning the treaty between Russia and China.
= 2035 Konsulatsarkiver. Shanghai. Korrespondancesager
m.v. 1842-94: Pakke 9, nr. 24.

22.

Date: (9 July 1860) - Hsien-feng 10, 5, 21.
From: Wu Hsü, Financial Commissioner, Shanghai.
To: James Whittall, Consul of Denmark, Shanghai.
Communication notifying the Consul that Hsüeh Huan has
been appointed Acting Governor-general of Kiangsu and
Kiangnan. Therefore Wu Hsü has been appointed Acting
Financial Commissioner of Kiangsu.
= 2035 Konsulatsarkiver. Shanghai. Korrespondancesager
m.v. 1842-94: Pakke 1, nr. 2.

23.

Date: (20 April 1861) - Hsien-feng, 11, 3, 11.
From: Wu Hsü, Acting Financial Commissioner, Shanghai.
To: James Whittall, Consul of Denmark, Shanghai.
Communication notifying that the Consul of Spain,
E. de Fortuny, is to travel to Canton. The Vice-Consul,
Domingo Munoz, assumes the responsibility temporarily.
= 2035 Konsulatsarkiver. Shanghai. Korrespondancesager
m.v. 1842-94: Pakke 9, nr. 13.

24.

Date: 26 April 1861. - Hsien-feng 11, 3, 17.
From: Wu Hsü, Acting Financial Commissioner, Shanghai.
To: James Whittall, Consul of Denmark, Shanghai.
Communication acknowledging that the Acting Consul of
Great Britain, Medhurst, assumes the post as Consul.
The previous Consul, T.T. Meadows, has retired.
= 2035 Konsulatsarkiver. Shanghai. Korrespondancesager
m.v. 1842-94: Pakke 9, nr. 14.

25.

Date: (4 May 1861) - Hsien-feng, 11, 3, 25.
From: Wu Hsü, Acting Financial Commissioner, Shanghai.
To: James Whittall, Consul of Denmark, Shanghai.
Communication acknowledging that R. Heinsen is appointed to the post of Consul of Bremen, previously under the authority of the Consul of Hamburg.
= 2035 Konsulatsarkiver. Shanghai. Korrespondancesager m.v. 1842-94: Pakke 9, nr. 3.

26.

Date: (21 June 1861) - Hsien-feng 11, 5, 14.
From: Wu Hsü, Acting Financial Commissioner, Shanghai.
To: James Whittall, Consul of Denmark, Shanghai.
Letter requesting that the Danish Consul translate an English visiting-card into Chinese.
= 2035 Konsulatsarkiver. Shanghai. Korrespondancesager m.v. 1842-94: Pakke 9, nr. 16.

27.

Date: 8 March 1862 - T'ung-chih 1, 2, 8.
From: Wu Hsü, Acting Financial Commissioner, Shanghai.
To: James Whittall, Consul of Denmark, Shanghai.
Communication acknowledging the appointment of the Consul of the United States of America, Smith, who assumes the post after the previous Consul, Seward.
= 2035 Konsulatsarkiver. Shanghai. Korrespondancesager m.v. 1842-94: Pakke 2, nr. 1.

28.

Date: (26 October 1862) - T'ung-chih, 1, 9, 4.
From: Wu Hsü, Acting Financial Commissioner, Shanghai.
To: James Whittall, Consul of Denmark, Shanghai.
Communication acknowledging the departure of the Consul of Oldenburg, W. Probst. The Acting Consul assumes responsibility temporarily.
= 2035 Konsulatsarkiver. Shanghai. Korrespondancesager m.v. 1842-94: Pakke 9, nr. 21.

29.

Date: (27 November 1862) - T'ung-Chih 1, 10, 6.
From: Huang Fang, Military Intendant, Shanghai.
To: James Whittall, Consul of Denmark, Shanghai.
Communication notifying the Consul that Huang Fang has been appointed to the post of Inspector of Customs at Shanghai in place of Wu Hsü.
= 2035 Konsulatsarkiver. Shanghai. Korrespondancesager m.v. 1842-94: Pakke 9, nr. 53.

30.

*Date: (7 February 1863) - T'ung-chih 1, 12, 20.
From: Huang Fang, Military Intendant, Shanghai.
To: James Whittall, Consul of Denmark, Shanghai.*
Communication in reply stating that the Danish Consul has no authority in the case against a Danish ship for illegal anchoring because there is no treaty between Denmark and China. The Consul should consult the Inspector-general of the Imperial Maritime Customs, G.H. Fitz-Roy, if he has further objections.
= 2035 Konsulatsarkiver. Shanghai. Korrespondancesager m.v. 1842-94: Pakke 9, nr. 11.

31.

*Date: (6 March 1863) - T'ung-chih 2, 1, 17.
From: Huang Fang, Military Intendant, Shanghai.
To: James Whittall, Consul of Denmark, Shanghai.*
Communication acknowledging the establishment of a Consulate-General of France at Shanghai. M.V.Mauboussin is appointed Consul-General.
= 2035 Konsulatsarkiver. Shanghai. Korrespondancesager m.v. 1842-94: Pakke 9, nr. 10.

32.

*Date: (24 March 1863) - T'ung-chih 2, 2, 6.
From: Huang Fang, Military Intendant, Shanghai.
To: James Whittall, Consul of Denmark, Shanghai.*
Communication stating that the Danish subject, Thomas Hansen, should be strictly interrogated in the case against him for protecting some contraband ammunition onboard a ship under charter from the American business firm, "Pao-lung".
= 2035 Konsulatsarkiver. Shanghai. Korrespondancesager m.v. 1842-94: Pakke 9, nr. 70.

33.

*Date: (2 April 1863) - T'ung-chih 2, 2, 15.
From: Huang Fang, Military Intendant, Shanghai.
To: James Whittall, Consul of Denmark, Shanghai.*
Communication acknowledging the appointment of the Consul of Great Britain.
= 2035 Konsulatsarkiver. Shanghai. Korrespondancesager m.v. 1842-94: Pakke 9, nr. 9.

34.

Date: (12 May 1863) - T'ung-chih 2, 3, 25.
From: Wu Hsü, Intendant, Shanghai.
To: James Whittall, Consul of Denmark, Shanghai.
Communication acknowledging that the Consul of Hamburg assumes the responsibility of the post of Consul of Lübeck. The previous Consul has retired.
= 2035 Konsulatsarkiver. Shanghai. Korrespondancesager m.v. 1842-94: Pakke 9, nr. 8.

35.

Date: (12 June 1863) - T'ung-chih 2, 4, 27.
From: Huang Fang, Military Intendant, Shanghai.
To: James Whittall, Consul of Denmark, Shanghai.
Communication acknowledging that the Consul of Great Britain has retired from the post. The Vice-Consul, J. Markham, assumes the responsibilities temporarily.
= 2035 Konsulatsarkiver. Shanghai. Korrespondancesager m.v. 1842-94: Pakke 9, nr. 2.

36.

Date:13 July 1863 - Kuei-hai year, 5, 28.
The original Treaty between Denmark and China with Tariff Regulations, in Chinese and English.
= 1649 Traktater. Kina. nr. 1.

37.

Date: 13 July 1863 - T'ung-chih 2, 5, 28.
Copy of Chinese version of the Treaty between China and Denmark, ratified by the Chinese Emperor.
= 1649 Traktater. Kina. nr. 5.

38.

Date: 13 July 1863 - T'ung-chih 2, 5, 28.
Copy of the Chinese version of the Treaty between China and Denmark.
= 1649 Traktater. Kina. nr. 2.

39.

Date: 13 July 1863 - T'ung chih 2, 5, 28.
Two copies of the Chinese version of the Tariff Regulations of the Treaty between China and Denmark.
= 1649 Traktater. Kina. nr. 3 + 4.

40.

Date: (1 August 1863) - T'ung-chih 2, 6, 17.
From: Huang Fang, Military Intendant, Shanghai.
To: James Whittall, Consul of Denmark, Shanghai.
Communication notifying the Consul that a Consulate-General of Sweden and Norway has been established in Shanghai.
= 2035 Konsulatsarkiver. Shanghai. Korrespondancesager m.v. 1842-94: Pakke 2, nr. 2.

41.

Date: (7 August 1863) - T'ung-chih 2, 6, 23.
From: Huang Fang, Military Intendant, Shanghai.
To: William Keswick, Consul of Denmark, Shanghai.
Communication in reply stating that the Consul of Denmark, James Whittall, has departed for home. It is acknowledged that the Acting Consul, William Keswick, will assume the responsibility temporarily.
= 2035 Konsulatsarkiver. Shanghai. Korrespondancesager m.v. 1842-94: Pakke 9, nr. 23.

42.

Date: (10 September 1863) - T'ung-chih 2, 7, 28.
From: Huang Fang, Military Intendant, Shanghai.
To: William Keswick, Consul of Denmark, Shanghai.
Communication in reply stating that no one of Danish nationality is among the four foreigners who were captured in company with the T'ai-P'ing rebels.
= 2035 Konsulatsarkiver. Shanghai. Korrespondancesager 1842-94: Pakke 9, nr. 40.

43.

Date: 11 November 1863 - T'ung-chih 2, 10, 1.
From: Huang Fang, Military Intendant, Shanghai.
To: William Keswick, Consul of Denmark, Shanghai.
Communication stating that the Consul-General of France, M.V. Mauboussin, has travelled to the Chusan Islands in order to recover from his illness. The Acting Consul, G.C. Rameau, assumes responsibility for the post temporarily.
= 2035 Konsulatsarkiver. Shanghai. Korrespondancesager. m.v. 1842-94: Pakke 2, nr. 3.

44.

Date: 30 December 1863 - T'ung-chih 2, 11, 20.
From: Huang Fang, Military Intendant, Shanghai.
To: William Keswick, Consul of Denmark, Shanghai.
Letter offering New Year Greetings from Huang Fang to the Consul. Huang Fang is unfortunately occupied with official business at the moment so that he has no opportunity to visit the Consulate.
= 2035 Konsulatsarkiver. Shanghai. Korrespondancesager m.v. 1842-94: Pakke 2, nr. 4.

45.

Date: 13 January 1864 - T'ung-chih 2, 12, 5.
From: Huang Fang, Military Intendant, Shanghai.
To: William Keswick, Consul of Denmark, Shanghai.
Communication notifying the Consul of the appointment of the Vice-consul of Spain, W.A. Rodriguez, to the post as Consul. The previous Consul, John Moore, has retired.
= 2035 Konsulatsarkiver. Shanghai. Korrespondancesager m.v. 1842-94: Pakke 3, nr. 1.

46.

Date: (24 January 1864) - T'ung-chih 2, 12, 16.
From: Huang Fang, Military Intendant, Shanghai.
To: William Keswick, Consul of Denmark, Shanghai.
Communication notifying the Consul of the appointment of the Prefect, Ying Pao-shi, as Attaché at the office of the Superintendant of Trade at the Southern Ports. Henceforth, both Huang Fang and Ying Pao-shih will supervise the trade affairs of Shanghai.
= 2035 Konsulatsarkiver. Shanghai. Korrespondancesager m.v. 1842-94: Pakke 9, nr. 52.

47.

Date: (24 January 1864) - T'ung-chih 2, 12, 16.
From: Huang Fang, Military Intendant, Shanghai.
To: William Keswick, Consul of Denmark, Shanghai.
Communication stating that Huang Fang is to travel to Nanking on official business.
= 2035 Konsulatsarkiver. Shanghai. Korrespondancesager m.v. 1842-94: Pakke 9, nr. 71.

48.

Date: (24 January 1864) - T'ung-chih 2, 12, 16.
From: Huang Fang, Military Intendant, Shanghai.
To: William Keswick, Consul of Denmark, Shanghai.
Communication acknowledging the appointment of the
Consul-General of Sweden and Norway, J.B. Forbes. The
previous Consul-General, Edward Cunningham, is to
travel home.
= 2035 Konsulatsarkiver. Shanghai. Korrespondancesager
m.v. 1842-94: Pakke 9, nr. 88.

49.

Date: (31 January 1864) - T'ung-chih 2, 12, 23.
From: Huang Fang, Military Intendant, Shanghai.
To: William Keswick, Consul of Denmark, Shanghai.
Communication stating that Huang Fang has returned from
a trip to Nanking on official business.
= 2035 Konsulatsarkiver. Shanghai. Korrespondancesager
m.v. 1842-94: Pakke 3, nr. 2.

50.

Date: 27 February 1864 - T'ung-chih 3, 1, 20.
From: Ying Pao-shih, Intendant, Shanghai.
To: William Keswick, Consul of Denmark, Shanghai.
Communication notifying the Consul of the appointment of
Ying Pao-shih as Intendant and Inspector of Customs in
Kiangsu, assuming the post after Huang Fang.
= 2035 Konsulatsarkiver. Shanghai. Korrespondancesager
m.v. 1842-94: Pakke 3, nr. 3.

51.

Date: (6 March 1864) - T'ung-chih 3, 1, 28.
From: Ying Pao-shih, Intendant, Shanghai.
To: William Keswick, Consul of Denmark, Shanghai.
Communication acknowledging the appointment of the Consul
of Great Britain, H.J. Parkes.
= 2035 Konsulatsarkiver. Shanghai. Korrespondancesager
m.v. 1842-94: Pakke 3, nr. 4.

52.

Date: (6 March 1864) - T'ung-chih 3, 1, 28.
From: Ying Pao-shih, Intendant, Shanghai.
To: William Keswick, Consul of Denmark, Shanghai.
Communication stating that Ying Pao-shih is to travel
to Nanking on official business.
= 2035 Konsulatsarkiver. Shanghai. Korrespondancesager
1842-94: Pakke 3, nr. 5.

53.

Date: 14 March 1864 - T'ung-chih 3, 2, 7.
From: Ying Pao-shih, Intendant, Shanghai.
To: William Keswick, Consul of Denmark, Shanghai.
Communication stating that Ying Pao-shih has returned
from a trip to Nanking on official business.
= 2035 Konsulatsarkiver. Shanghai. Korrespondancesager
m.v. 1842-94: Pakke 3, nr. 6.

54.

Date: 4 April 1864 - T'ung-chih 3, 2, 28.
From: Ying Pao-shih, Intendant, Shanghai.
To: William Keswick, Consul of Denmark, Shanghai.
Communication acknowledging the appointment of the
Consul of Hamburg, R. Heinsen, who recently has returned
from a trip to his home, to the additional post as
Consul of Lübeck and Bremen. The previous Consul has
returned home.
= 2035 Konsulatsarkiver. Shanghai. Korrespondancesager
m.v. 1842-94: Pakke 3, nr. 7.

55.

Date: 16 April 1864 - T'ung-chih 3, 3, 11.
From: Ying Pao-shih, Intendant, Shanghai.
To: William Keswick, Consul of Denmark, Shanghai.
Communication acknowledging the appointment of the
Consul of Spain, Eusebio de Fortuny.
= 2035 Konsulatsarkiver. Shanghai. Korrespondancesager
m.v. 1842-94: Pakke 3, nr. 8.

56.

Date: (23 April 1864) - T'ung-chih 3, 3, 18.
From: Ying Pao-shih, Intendant, Shanghai.
To: William Keswick, Consul of Denmark, Shanghai.
Communication acknowledging the appointment of the
Acting Consul-General of France and the appointment of
the Vice-Consul of France.
= 2035 Konsulatsarkiver. Shanghai. Korrespondancesager
m.v. 1842-94: Pakke 3, nr. 9.

57.

Date: 13 June 1864 - T'ung-chih 3, 5, 10.
From: Ying Pao-shih, Intendant, Shanghai.
To: William Keswick, Consul of Denmark, Shanghai.
Communication notifying the Consul of the appointment
of the Consul-General of Portugal.
= 2035 Konsulatsarkiver. Shanghai. Korrespondancesager
m.v. 1842-94: Pakke 3, nr. 10.

58.

Date: (16 June 1864) - T'ung-chih 3, 5, 13.
From: Ying Pao-shih, Intendant, Shanghai.
To: William Keswick, Consul of Denmark, Shanghai.
Communication notifying the Consul of the appointment
of the Consul of Prussia as Acting Consul-General.
= 2035 Konsulatsarkiver. Shanghai. Korrespondancesager
m.v. 1842-94: Pakke 3, nr. 11.

59.

Date: (9 July 1864) - T'ung chih 3, 6, 6.
From: Ch'ung-hou, Superintendant of Trade at the Northern
      Ports, Tientsin.
To: Steen Andersen Bille, Danish Envoy, Tientsin.
Communication stating that on account of the arrival of the
Danish Envoy, Steen Andersen Bille, to Tientsin to exchange
the treaties ratified between Denmark and China, the English
Secretary Thomas Wade has requested that appropriate Chinese
officials can be appointed to carry out the exchange. Consequently Li Heng-sung and Liu Hsün-kao have been commissioned
by the Chinese Emperor to exchange treaties at Shanghai.
The Danish Envoy is therefore requested to return to Shanghai
and contact the Chinese authorities there.
= 5154 Privatarkiver. Admiral Steen Andersen Bille's (+1883)
Arkiv: Sager vedr. St. Billes Gesantskabsreise til Kina
1864, nr. 3.

60.

Date: (25 July 1864) - T'ung-chih 3, 6, 22.
From: Ting Jih-ch'ang, Military Intendant, Shanghai.
To: William Koswick, Consul of Denmark, Shanghai.
Communication stating that appropriate action has been taken
relating to the arrival of the Danish Envoy, Steen Andersen
Bille, to Shanghai to exchange the ratified treaties between
Denmark and China.
= 2035 Konsulatsarkiver. Shanghai. Korrespondancesager
m.v. 1842-94: Pakke 3, nr. 12.

61.

Date: (26 July 1864) - T'ung-chih 3, 6, 23.
From: Li Heng-sung, Commander in chief, Nanking + Liu
      Hsün-kao, Financial Commissioner, Suchou.
To: Steen Andersen Bille, Danish Envoy, Shanghai.
Communication stating that a despatch has been received from
the Intendant of Shanghai, Ting Jih-ch'ang, notifying the
officials of the arrival of the Danish Envoy, Steen Andersen
Bille, to Shanghai to exchange treaties. Consequently the
appropriate authorities have been informed and the residence
of the Governor of Kiangsu has been chosen as the place
where the exchange of ratified treaties will take place.
= 5154 Privatarkiver. Admiral Steen Andersen Bille's (+1883)
Arkiv: Sager vedr. St. Billes Gesantskabsreise til Kina
1864, nr. 1.

62.

Date: (29 July 1864) - T'ung-chih 3, 6, 26.
*From: Li Heng-sung, Commander-in-chief, Nanking + Liu
     Hsün-kao, Financial Commissioner, Suchou.*
To: Steen Andersen Bille, Danish Envoy, Shanghai.
Communication stating that on account of the emergency
created by the outbreak of a war between Denmark and
Prussia the Danish Envoy, Steen Andersen Bille, would
like to finish the exchange of the ratified treaties as
quickly as possible. Subsequently the Chinese authorities
have agreed to exchange the treaties on 29th July, at
five o'clock, at the residence of the Governor of Kiangsu,
Li Hung-chang.
= 5154 Privatarkiver. Admiral Steen Andersen Bille's
(+1883) Arkiv: Sager vedr. St. Billes Gesantskabsreise
til Kina 1864, nr. 2.

63.

Date: (July 1864) - T'ung-chih 3, 4, -.
*From: Li Heng-sung, Commander-in-chief, Nanking + Liu
     Hsün-kao, Financial Commissioner, Suchou.*
To: Steen Andersen Bille, Danish Envoy, Shanghai.
Communication stating that Li Heng-sung and Liu Hsün-kao
have exchanged the treaty ratified by the Emperor of
China with the treaty ratified by the Danish King, brought
to China by the Danish Envoy, Steen Andersen Bille. Now
that the Treaty between Denmark and China has been
ratified by both countries, there should be hope for a
peaceful friendship in the future.
= 1646 Traktater. Kina. Letter.

64.

Date: 4 August 1864 - T'ung-chih 3, 7, 3.
From: Steen Andersen Bille, Danish Envoy, Shanghai.
To: Tsungli Yamen, Peking.
Communication requesting that the Chinese authorities
will provide sufficient protection to Danish ships
which are attacked by Prussian warships at Chinese
ports. Reference is made to the recently ratified Treaty
between Denmark and China and to a proclamation from the
British Government.
Appended: A copy of a translation of the proclamation
issued by the British Governor of Hongkong concerning the
war between Denmark and Prussia.
= 2035 Konsulatsarkiver. Shanghai. Korrespondancesager
m.v. 1842-94: Pakke 3, nr. 13.

65.

Date: 26 August 1864 - T'ung-chih 3, 7, 25.
From: Ting Jih-ch'ang, Military Intendant, Shanghai.
To: William Keswick, Consul of Denmark, Shanghai.
Communication stating that Ting Jih-ch'ang is to travel to Nanking on official business.
= 2035 Konsulatsarkiver. Shanghai. Korrespondancesager m.v. 1842-94: Pakke 3, nr. 14.

66.

Date: 30 August 1864 - T'ung-chih 3, 7, 29.
From: Ting Jih-ch'ang, Military Intendant, Shanghai.
To: William Keswick, Consul of Denmark, Shanghai.
Communication stating that Ting Jih-ch'ang has returned to his post after a trip to Nanking on official business.
= 2035 Konsulatsarkiver. Shanghai. Korrespondancesager m.v. 1842-94: Pakke 3, nr. 15.

67.

Date: (3 September 1864) - T'ung-chih 3, 8, 3.
From: Li Hung-chang, Governor of Kiangsu, Nanking.
To: Steen Andersen Bille, Danish Envoy, Shanghai.
Communication stating that the official Chinese translation of the ratified Treaty between Denmark and China will be forwarded to the Chinese Emperor only after the title of the Danish sovereign has been changed from Emperor to King and the article on correspondence between a Danish Ambassador and the Chinese authorities has been changed to follow the usual procedure.
= 2035 Konsulatsarkiver. Shanghai. Korrespondancesager m.v. 1842-94: Pakke 9, nr. 82.

68.

Date: (22 September 1864) - T'ung-chih 3, 8, 22.
From: Ting Jih-ch'ang, Military Intendant, Shanghai.
To: William Keswick, Consul of Denmark, Shanghai.
Communication acknowledging that J.B. Forbes has been appointed Consul-General of Sweden and Norway.
= 2035 Konsulatsarkiver. Shanghai. Korrespondancesager m.v. 1842-94: Pakke 3, nr. 16.

69.

Date: 8 October 1864 - T'ung-chih 3, 9, 8.
From: Ting Jih-ch'ang, Military Intendant, Shanghai.
To: William Keswick, Consul of Denmark, Shanghai.
Communication stating that Ting-Jih-ch'ang is to travel to Nanking on official business.
= 2035 Konsulatsarkiver. Shanghai. Korrespondancesager m.v. 1842-94: Pakke 3, nr. 17.

70.

Date: 14 October 1864 - T'ung-chih 3, 9, 14.
From: Ting Jih-ch'ang, Military Intendant, Shanghai.
To: William Keswick, Consul of Denmark, Shanghai.
Communication stating that Ting Jih-ch'ang has returned
to his post after a trip to Nanking on official business.
= 2035 Konsulatsarkiver. Shanghai. Korrespondancesager
m.v. 1842-94: Pakke 3, nr. 18.

71.

Date: 17 November 1864 - T'ung-chih 3, 10, 19.
From: Ting Jih-ch'ang, Military Intendant, Shanghai.
To: William Keswick, Consul of Denmark, Shanghai.
Communication stating that regulations should be drawn
up which could eliminate the gambling-houses at the
Foreign Settlement of Shanghai. The Consul is requested
to present his suggestions on the subject.
= 2035 Konsulatsarkiver. Shanghai. Korrespondancesager
m.v. 1842-94: Pakke 3, nr. 19.

72.

Date: (14 December 1864) - T'ung-chih 3, 11, 16.
From: Ting Jih-ch'ang, Military Intendant, Shanghai.
To: William Keswick, Consul of Denmark, Shanghai.
Communication stating that after the 1st January 1865,
the Customs drawbacks will only be repaid within a time-
limit of 10 days after the vessel on which the goods were
exported has received its port clearance.
= 2035 Konsulatsarkiver. Shanghai. Korrespondancesager
m.v. 1842-94: Pakke 3, nr. 20.

73.

Date: 25 December 1864 - T'ung-chih 3, 11, 28.
From: Ting Jih-ch'ang, Military Intendant, Shanghai.
To: William Keswick, Consul of Denmark, Shanghai.
Communication acknowledging the appointment of the Consul-
General of France, who assumes the responsibility of the
post from the previous Acting Consul-General.
= 2035 Konsulatsarkiver. Shanghai. Korrespondancesager
m.v. 1842-94: Pakke 3, nr. 21.

74.

Date: (30 December 1864) - T'ung-chih 3, 12, 2.
From: Ting Jih-ch'ang, Military Intendant, Shanghai.
To: William Keswick, Consul of Denmark, Shanghai.
Letter announcing that the Chinese officials of Shanghai
will visit the Danish Consulate on New Year's Day to
offer their New Year Greetings.
= 2035 Konsulatsarkiver. Shanghai. Korrespondancesager
m.v. 1842-94: Pakke 9, nr. 18.

75.

Date: (1 January 1865) - T'ung-chih 3, 12, 4.
From: Ting Jih-ch'ang, Military Intendant, Shanghai.
To: William Keswick, Consul of Denmark, Shanghai.
Communication stating that Ting Jih-ch'ang is to travel away on official business.
= 2035 Konsulatsarkiver. Shanghai. Korrespondancesager m.v. 1842-94: Pakke 4, nr. 1.

76.

Date: (7 January 1865) - T'ung-chih 3, 12, 10.
From: Ting Jih-ch'ang, Military Intendant, Shanghai.
To: William Keswick, Consul of Denmark, Shanghai.
Communication stating that Ting Jih-ch'ang has returned from a trip to the interior of China.
= 2035 Konsulatsarkiver. Shanghai. Korrespondancesager m.v. 1842-94: Pakke 9, nr. 87.

77.

Date: 19 January 1865 - T'ung-chih 3, 12, 22.
From: Ting Jih-ch'ang, Military Intendant, Shanghai.
To: William Keswick, Consul of Denmark, Shanghai.
Communication stating that Ting Jih-ch'ang is to travel away on official business.
= 2035 Konsulatsarkiver. Shanghai. Korrespondancesager m.v. 1842-94: Pakke 4, nr. 3.

78.

Date: 5 May 1865 - T'ung-chih 4, 4, 11.
From: Wang, Acting Prefect, Shanghai.
To: Office of the Mixed Court, Shanghai.
Communication stating that the case against the foreigners who have robbed several Chinese subjects on board a boat crossing the river should be dealt with severity, because the evidence gives definite proof that they are guilty.
= 2035 Konsulatsarkiver. Shanghai. Korrespondancesager m.v. 1842-94: Pakke 4, nr. 5.

79.

Date: (8 May 1865) - T'ung-chih 4, 4, 14.
From: Ting Jih-ch'ang, Military Intendant, Shanghai.
To: William Keswick, Consul of Denmark, Shanghai.
Communication notifying that Ting Jih-ch'ang is to travel away on official business.
= 2035 Konsulatsarkiver. Shanghai. Korrespondancesager m.v. 1842-94: Pakke 4, nr. 31.

80.

Date: 15 May 1865 - T'ung-chih 4, 4, 21.
From: Ting Jih-ch'ang, Military Intendant, Shanghai.
To: William Keswick, Consul of Denmark, Shanghai.
Communication in reply stating that a petition has been received from a Chinese subject, A Mao, requesting that the owner of the Danish business firm "Wang-fu", Mr. Stephen, be brought to trial on account of his debts.
Appended: A copy of the petition from A Mao.
= 2035 Konsulatsarkiver. Shanghai. Korrespondancesager m.v. 1842-94: Pakke 4, nr. 6.

81.

Date: (21 May 1865) - T'ung-chih 4, 4, 27.
From: Hsü, Expectant Intendant, Shanghai.
To: William Keswick, Consul of Denmark, Shanghai.
Communication stating that the case against the owner of the Danish business firm "Wang-fu", Mr. Stephen, is to be heard at the Magistrate's office on the 23rd May.
= 2035 Konsulatsarkiver. Shanghai. Korrespondancesager m.v. 1842-94: Pakke 9, nr. 29.

82.

Date: 5 July 1865 - T'ung-chih 4, Jun5, 13.
From: Wang, Prefect, Shanghai.
To: William Keswick, Consul of Denmark.
Communication stating that the two Chinese plaintiffs in the case against four foreigners for robbery have not been able to attend court because they live at a remote place and the roads have not been passable due to heavy rainfall. Officials have been sent to summon them.
= 2035 Konsulatsarkiver. Shanghai. Korrespondancesager m.v. 1842-94: Pakke 4, nr. 7.

83.

Date: 11 July 1865 - T'ung-chih 4, Jun5, 19.
From: Wang, Prefect, Shanghai.
To: William Keswick, Consul of Denmark, Shanghai.
Communication stating that the two Chinese plaintiffs in the case against four foreigners for robbery have not been able to attend court because one of them is ill and the other has recently travelled abroad. Furthermore the Consul of Great Britain has notified the Chinese authorities that the case against the British defendants can be settled at once without the participation of the plaintiffs,
= 2035 Konsulatsarkiver. Shanghai. Korrespondancesager m.v. 1842-94: Pakke 4, nr. 8.

84.

Date: 14 February 1866 - T'ung-chih 4, 12, 29.
From: Ying Pao-shih, Military Intendant, Shanghai.
To: William Keswick, Consul of Denmark, Shanghai.
Letter inviting the Consul to visit the Chinese officials at Shanghai at the office of the Military Intendant to offer his greetings on the Chinese New Year.
= 2035 Konsulatsarkiver. Shanghai. Korrespondancesager m.v. 1842-94: Pakke 4, nr. 9.

85.

Date: 19 February 1866 - T'ung-chih 5, 1, 2.
From: Ying Pao-shih, Military Intendant, Shanghai.
To: William Keswick, Consul of Denmark, Shanghai.
Communication stating that Ying Pao-shih is to travel away on official business.
= 2035 Konsulatsarkiver. Shanghai. Korrespondancesager m.v. 1842-94: Pakke 4, nr. 10.

86.

Date: 23 February 1866 - T'ung-chih 5, 1, 9.
From: Ying Pao-shih, Military Intendant, Shanghai.
To: William Keswick, Consul of Denmark, Shanghai.
Communication stating that Ying Pao-shih has returned to his post after a trip on official business.
= 2035 Konsulatsarkiver. Shanghai. Korrespondancesager m.v. 1842-94: Pakke 4, nr. 11.

87.

Date: 3 May 1866 - T'ung-chih 5, 3, 19.
From: Ying Pao-shih, Military Intendant, Shanghai.
To: William Keswick, Consul of Denmark, Shanghai.
Communication notifying the Consul that the Inspector-General of the Imperial Maritime Customs, Robert Hart, has left for Europe on a vacation. Thus G.H. Fitz-Roy will act as the Inspector-General during his absence.
= 2035 Konsulatsarkiver. Shanghai. Korrespondancesager m.v. 1842-94: Pakke 4, nr. 12.

88.

Date: (22 May 1866) - T'ung-chih 5, 4, 9.
From: Ying Pao-shih, Military Intendant, Shanghai.
To: William Keswick, Consul of Denmark, Shanghai.
Communication acknowledging the appointment of the Consul-General of France to the concurrent post as Consul of Spain. The previous Consul of Spain, M.B. de Rablez, has returned to Spain.
= 2035 Konsulatsarkiver. Shanghai. Korrespondancesager m.v. 1842-94: Pakke 4, nr. 13.

89.

Date: (15 June 1866) - T'ung-chih 5, 5, 3.
From: Ying Pao-shih, Military Intendant, Shanghai.
To: William Keswick, Consul of Denmark, Shanghai.
Communication stating that according to Imperial orders, a copy of the Emigration Act of 1866, which was negotiated between China, Great Britain and France, should be forwarded to all foreign Consuls. Therefore a copy is enclosed.
= 2035 Konsulatsarkiver. Shanghai. Korrespondancesager m.v. 1842-94: Pakke 4, nr. 14.

90.

Hsü-ting Chao-kung Chang-cheng T'iao-yüeh:
Convention to Regulate the Engagement of Chinese Emigrants by British and French subjects. Signed 5 March 1866. Movable-type printing 1866.
See: Mayers, W.F.: "Treaties between the Empire of China and Foreign Powers" Shanghai 1902. Page 32 ff.
= 2035 Konsulatsarkiver. Shanghai. Korrespondancesager m.v. 1842-94: Pakke 9, nr. 92.

91.

Date: 7 August 1866 - T'ung-chih 5, 6, 27.
From: Ying Pao-shih, Military Intendant, Shanghai.
To: William Keswick, Consul of Denmark, Shanghai.
Communication in reply expressing grief at the news of the departure of William Keswick, who has retired from the post as Consul of Denmark. In addition acknowledging the appointment of Edward Whittall to the post as Consul of Denmark.
= 2035 Konsulatsarkiver. Shanghai. Korrespondancesager 1842-94: Pakke 4, nr. 15.

92.

Date: (21 September 1866) - T'ung-chih 5, 8, 13.
From: Ying Pao-shih, Military Intendant, Shanghai.
To: Edward Whittall, Consul of Denmark, Shanghai.
Communication notifying the Consul that the time-limit for declaration of duty-free, water-damaged opium at the Chinese customs has been fixed at ten days.
= 2035 Konsulatsarkiver. Shanghai. Korrespondancesager m.v. 1842-94: Pakke 9, nr. 30.

93.

Date: 2 October 1866 - Kuang-hsü 12, 9, 5.
From: Liao, Expectant Sub-Prefect, Swatow.
To: Walter Allum, Consul of Denmark, Swatow.
Communication acknowledging the appointment of the
Consul of Denmark, Walter Allum.
= 2120 Konsulatsarkiver. Swatow. Indkomne breve
1894-1912 nr. 15.

94.

Date: (30 December 1866) - T'ung-chih 5, 11, 24.
From: Ying Pao-shih, Military Intendant, Shanghai.
To: Edward Whittall, Consul of Denmark, Shanghai.
Letter offering New Year Greetings. Ying Pao-shih is
preoccupied by urgent business matters at the moment
and is therefore unable to visit the Consulate.
= 2035 Konsulatsarkiver. Shanghai. Korrespondancesager
m.v. 1842-94: Pakke 4, nr. 16.

95.

Date: (22 November 1867) - T'ung-chih 6, 10, 12.
From: Tsungli Yamen, Peking.
To: C.E. Krag-Juel-Vind-Frijs, Minister of Foreign
    Affairs, Copenhagen.
Communication stating that an Imperial Edict of the 20th
November 1867 commissions A. Burlinghame, the retired
ambassador of the United States of America at Peking,
with the power to act as Minister Plenipotentiary for
China in a mission to the Western nations.
= 239 A.J. nr. 1206-7874. Samlede sager. Handelstraktat
med Kina 1864-1904: C.nr. 1.

96.

Date: (27 November 1867) - T'ung-chih 6, 11, 2.
From: Tsungli Yamen, Peking.
To: C.E. Krag-Juel-Vind-Frijs, Minister of Foreign
    Affairs, Copenhagen.
Communication stating that in accordance with an Imperial
Edict of the 26th November 1867, the Chinese High
Ministers of the Tsungli Yamen, Chih-Kang and Sun
Chia-ku, have been commissioned as advisors to
A. Burlinghame on the Chinese mission to the Western
nations. For this purpose they have both been conferred
with a rank of the second grade, Sun Chia-ku furthermore
being allowed to wear the Peacock Feather Emblem.
= 239 A.J. nr. 1206-7874. Samlede sager. Handelstraktat
med Kina 1864-1904: C.nr. 2.

97.

Date: (27 November 1867) - T'ung-chih 6, 11, 2.
From: Tsungli Yamen, Peking.
To: C.E. Krag-Juel-Vind-Frijs, Minister of Foreign
    Affairs, Copenhagen.
Communication stating that in accordance with an Imperial Edict of 26th November 1867, John McLarvy Brown has been appointed First Secretary and de Champs has been appointed Second Secretary to the Chinese mission to the Western nations.
= 239 A.J. nr. 1206-7874. Samlede sager. Handelstraktat med Kina 1864-1904: C. nr. 3.

98.

Date: (7 December 1867) - T'ung-chih 6, 11, 12.
From: Tsungli Yamen, Peking.
To: C.E. Krag-Juel-Vind-Frijs, Minister of Foreign
    Affairs, Copenhagen.
Communication stating that the Tsungli Yamen has decided to send A. Burlinghame as the Minister Plenipotentiary of the Chinese mission to Denmark and other Western nations. In co-ordination with the High Ministers Chi-kang and Sun Chia-ku he is to deliberate on all problems concerning the friendly relationship between Denmark and China and then report to the Tsungli Yamen.
= 239 A.J. nr. 1206-7874. Samlede sager. Handelstraktat med Kina 1864-1904: E.L.

99.

Date: (1874).
From: Chang Ch'i-ch'uai, Fuchou.
To: William Lemann, Acting Consul of Denmark, Fuchou.
Letter notifying the Consul of the appointment of Chang Ch'i-ch'uai to the post as Inspector at the Board of Trade. Inspector Chao has been transferred to manage the military affairs.
= 2035 Konsulatsarkiver. Shanghai. Korrespondancesager m.v. 1842-94: Pakke 9, nr. 66.

100.

Date: (1874).
From: Board of Trade, Fuchou.
To: W.S. Young, Vice-Consul of Denmark, Fuchou.
Letter stating that before the passports can be issued to the Danish employees of the Great Northern Telegraph Company, the Consul must correct the inconsistency of the names on one of the passports and supply more information as to where the Danes will travel.
= 2035 Konsulatsarkiver. Shanghai. Korrespondancesager m.v. 1842-94: Pakke 9, nr. 76.

101.

Date: (14 June 1874). - T'ung-chih 13, 5, 1.
From: Li Ho-nien, Governor-General + Wen-Yü, Commander-
    in-Chief, Fuchou.
Proclamation announcing that the Portuguese Emperor has
abolished the Chinese emigration from Macao. Hereafter,
it is strictly prohibited everywhere in China to engage
Chinese workers and sail them to foreign countries.
= 2035 Konsulatsarkiver. Shanghai. Korrespondancesager
m.v. 1842-94: Pakke 9, nr. 90.

102.

Date: (3 July 1874) - T'ung-chih 13, 5, 20.
From: Board of Trade, Fuchou.
To: William Leman, Acting Consul of Denmark, Fuchou.
Communication requesting the Consul to put up two copies
of the proclamation on the abolishment of Chinese
emigration from Macao at the Consulate, so that all
foreign merchants become acquainted with it.
= 2035 Konsulatsarkiver. Shanghai. Korrespondancesager
m.v. 1842-94: Pakke 9, nr. 65.

103.

Date: (1 August 1874) - (T'ung-chih 13), 6, 19.
From: Lu Hsin-yüan, Intendant, Fuchou.
To: M.M. DeLano, Acting Consul of Denmark, Fuchou.
Copy of a letter stating that Lu Hsin-yüan gives the
Great Northern Telegraph Company the permission to
construct a telegraph-line between Fuchou and Amoy.
However, because the distance covered by the line is
quite long and the work will take some time, the Intendant
has commissioned a Prefect, Chou, to survey the route
together with an officer of the Company so that detailed
plans can be made before commencing with the construction.
= Store Nordiske Arkiv: Stationskasse. Foochow-Amoy
Landlinier.

104.

Date: (4 September 1874) - T'ung-chih 13, 7, 24.
From: P'an Chün-chang, Fuchou.
To: William Leman, Acting Consul of Denmark, Fuchou.
Communication notifying the Consul of the appointment of
P'an Chün-chang as Assistant Commissioner to the Board of
Trade, because the Intendant, Lu Hsin-yüan is to travel
to Peking for an audience.
= 2035 Konsulatsarkiver. Shanghai. Korrespondancesager
m.v. 1842-94: Pakke 9, nr. 58.

105.

Date: 29 September 1874 - T'ung-chih 13, 8, 19.
From: Li Ho-nien, Governor-General, Fuchou.
To: W.G. Price, Consul of Denmark, Fuchou.
Copy of communication in reply stating that local officials have reported that the work on the Fuchou-Amoy telegraph-line ceased on account of the resistance of the common people. The Consul is requested to ask the Great Northern Telegraph Company to postpone the construction until the whole matter has been negotiated again.
= 2035 Konsulatsarkiver. Shanghai. Korrespondancesager m.v. 1842-94: Pakke 6, nr. 1.

106.

Date: (7 November 1874) - (T'ung-chih 13), 9, 29.
From: Board of Trade, Fuchou.
To: Consul of Denmark, Fuchou.
Copy of a letter requesting the Great Northern Telegraph Company to halt the construction of the Fuchou-Amoy telegraph-line and remove the erected telegraph-poles and wires because the local officials are not able to protect them if mobs of common people riot and destroy the lines.
= 2035 Konsulatsarkiver. Shanghai. Korrespondancesager m.v. 1842-94: Pakke 6, nr. 2.

107.

Date: (26 November 1874) - (T'ung-chih 13), 10, 18.
From: Board of Trade, Fuchou.
To: W.S. Young, Vice-Consul of Denmark, Fuchou.
Letter in reply stating that the deeds of the property purchased by the Great Northern Telegraph Company will be officially stamped after the necessary inquiries have been made.
= 2035 Konsulatsarkiver. Shanghai. Korrespondancesager m.v. 1842-94: Pakke 6, nr. 3.

108.

Date: (29 November 1874) - (T'ung-chih 13), 10, 21.
From: Board of Trade, Fuchou.
To: Consul of Denmark, Fuchou.
Copy of a letter stating that reports have been received concerning the plundering of the Fuchou-Amoy telegraph-line. It is impossible to protect the line and therefore the Great Northern Telegraph Company should cease the construction until a new agreement has been concluded. If they do not cease immediately, the Board of Trade will not be responsible if more trouble should occur.
= 2035 Konsulatsarkiver. Shanghai. Korrespondancesager m.v. 1842-94: Pakke 6, nr. 4.

109.

Date: (7 December 1874) - (T'ung-chih 13), 10, 29.
From: Board of Trade, Fuchou.
To: Consul of Denmark, Fuchou.
Copy of a letter stating that the Great Northern Telegraph Company have built the telegraph-line from Fuchou towards Amoy without permission from the Board of Trade. The common people are hostile towards the Great Northern Telegraph Company and have not been provoked by P'an Kuang-ch'ü as the Company maintains. The Great Northern Telegraph Company should remove the telegraph-poles etc. and await new negotiations.
= 2035 Konsulatsarkiver. Shanghai. Korrespondancesager m.v. 1842-94: Pakke 6, nr. 9.

110.

Date: 9 December 1874 - T'ung-chih 13, 11, 1.
From: W.S. Young, Vice-Consul of Denmark, Fuchou.
To: Board of Trade, Fuchou.
Copy of a communication stating that the Board of Trade has in fact already given its official consent to the construction of the Fuchou-Amoy telegraph-line. Therefore they should fulfil their part of the contract by punishing P'an Kuang-ch'ü, a local litteratus, for inciting trouble by circulating an anti-foreign placard, a copy of which is appended. Furthermore, according to articles 7 and 10 of the Treaty between Denmark and China all communication between the Board of Trade and the Danish Consul should be of an official nature.
= 2035 Konsulatsarkiver. Shanghai. Korrespondancesager m.v. 1842-94: Pakke 6, nr. 5.

111.

Date: 16 December 1874 - (T'ung-chih 13), 11, 8.
From: Board of Trade, Fuchou.
To: Consul of Denmark, Fuchou.
Letter stating that Henningsen's passport has been duly stamped and is returned enclosed.
= 2035 Konsulatsarkiver. Shanghai. Korrespondancesager m.v. 1842-94: Pakke 6, nr. 6.

112.

Date: 22 December 1874 - (T'ung-chih 13), 11, 14.
From: Board of Trade, Fuchou.
To: W.S. Young, Vice-Consul of Denmark, Fuchou.
Letter stating that the passports of Dreyer, Hoskier and Bojesen have been duly stamped and are returned enclosed.
= 2035 Konsulatsarkiver. Shanghai. Korrespondancesager m.v. 1842-94: Pakke 6, nr. 7.

113.

Date: 27 December 1874 - (T'ung-chih 13), 11, 19.
From: Board of Trade, Fuchou.
To: Consul of Denmark, Fuchou.
Letter stating that the passports have been duly stamped and are returned enclosed.
= 2035 Konsulatsarkiver. Shanghai. Korrespondancesager m.v. 1842-94: Pakke 6, nr. 8.

114.

Date: (1875?)
A list of the names and titles of all the Chinese officials in Fuchou.
= 2035 Konsulatsarkiver. Shanghai. Korrespondancesager m.v. 1842-94: Pakke 9, nr. 42.

115.

Date: (1875).
From: Shen Pao-chen, Fuchou.
To: W.S. Young, Vice-Consul of Denmark, Fuchou.
Letter requesting the Consul to translate the communications from the Danish Envoy, Waldemar Rudolf RaaslØff, as the Danish interpreter Shultz has left Fuchou.
= 1039 Konsulatsarkiver. Foochow. Indkomne breve m.m. 1862-93: nr. 45.

116.

Date: (1875).
From: Board of Trade, Fuchou.
To: W.S. Young, Vice-Consul of Denmark, Fuchou.
Letter stating that five promissory notes for a large sum of money plus two notebooks have been stolen from the Chinese business firm "Hung-hsing". Foreign firms are warned against buying them.
= 2035 Konsulatsarkiver. Shanghai. Korrespondancesager m.v. 1842-94: Pakke 9, nr. 68.

117.

Date: 2 January 1875 - (T'ung-chih 13), 11, 25.
From: Lin Ch'ing-yi, Fuchou.
To: W.S. Young, Vice-Consul of Denmark, Fuchou.
Letter stating that the deeds for the property purchased by the Great Northern Telegraph Company cannot be legally stamped before the court has decided whether or not the property is a stolen graveyard.
= 2035 Konsulatsarkiver. Shanghai. Korrespondancesager m.v. 1842-94: Pakke 6, nr. 10.

118.

Date: (11 January 1875) - T'ung-chih 13, 12, 4.
From: Tsungli Yamen, Peking.
To: Waldemar Rudolf Raasl∅ff, Ambassador of Denmark, Peking.
Part of a copy of a communication concerning the protection of the telegraph-line between Fuchou and Amoy.
= 2035 Konsulatsarkiver. Shanghai. Korrespondancesager m.v. 1842-94: Pakke 6, nr. 18.

119.

Date: 22 January 1875 - (T'ung-chih 13), 12, 15.
From: P'an Chün-chang, Fuchou.
To: W.S. Young, Vice-Consul of Denmark, Fuchou.
Letter stating that on account of a recent case of a Russian missionary travelling in the interior of China without a passport, all Consulates should inform their subjects that proper protection can only be given if they notify in advance to the Chinese authorities what their travel-plans are.
= 2035 Konsulatsarkiver. Shanghai. Korrespondancesager m.v. 1842-94: Pakke 6, nr. 11.

120.

Date: 23 January 1875 - (T'ung-chih 13), 12, 16.
From: Ting Chia-wei, Fuchou.
To: W.S. Young, Vice-Consul of Denmark, Fuchou.
Copy of a letter stating that Ting Chia-wei has been appointed Inspector at the Board of Trade in Fuchou.
= 2035 Konsulatsarkiver. Shanghai. Korrespondancesager m.v. 1842-94: Pakke 6, nr. 12.

121.

Date: (26 January 1875) - (T'ung-chih 13), 12, 19.
From: Board of Trade, Fuchou.
To: Consul of Denmark, Fuchou.
Copy of a letter in reply stating that communications have been received from the Consul stating that it is the opinion of the Great Northern Telegraph Company that it is the authorities and not the common people that prevent the construction of the Fuchou-Amoy telegraph-line. It is, on the contrary, the opinion of the Board of Trade that the Great Northern Telegraph Company is responsible for the disturbances as they have proceeded with the construction despite the warnings from the Board of Trade. The Great Northern Telegraph Company is requested to halt the construction of the telegraph-line immediately.
= 2035 Konsulatsarkiver. Shanghai. Korrespondancesager m.v. 1842-94: Pakke 9, nr. 48.

122.

Date: 4 February 1875.
From: Board of Trade, Fuchou.
To: W.S. Young, Vice-Consul of Denmark, Fuchou.
Copy of a letter stating that it is impossible to protect the Fuchou-Amoy telegraph-line. Hence, the Great Northern Telegraph Company should halt the construction of the line.
= 2035 Konsulatsarkiver. Shanghai. Korrespondancesager m.v. 1842-94: Pakke 9, nr. 44.

123.

Date: 13 February 1875.
From: W.S. Young, Vice-Consul of Denmark, Fuchou.
To: Board of Trade, Fuchou.
Copy of a letter stating that yesterday two Danes, employed by the Great Northern Telegraph Company, were attacked by Chinese soldiers who were disguised as a common mob and who tried to kill the Danes and burn down the watchhouse. The local officials who are inciting these disturbances should be prosecuted.
= 2035 Konsulatsarkiver. Shanghai. Korrespondancesager m.v. 1842-94: Pakke 9, nr. 45.

124.

Date: 13 February 1875 - (Kuang-hsü 1), 1, 8.
From: W.S. Young, Vice-Consul of Denmark, Fuchou.
To: Board of Trade, Fuchou.
Copy of a communication stating that local officials at Fang-k'ou have provoked disturbances that almost cost the lives of two Danes. The request is made that these officials be caught and dealt with severely according to articles 16 and 18 of the Treaty between Denmark and China.
= 2035 Konsulatsarkiver. Shanghai. Korrespondancesager m.v. 1842-94: Pakke 9, nr. 91.

125.

Date: 16 February 1875 - (Kuang-hsü 1), 1, 11.
From: Board of Trade, Fuchou.
To: Consul of Denmark, Fuchou.
Copy of a letter in reply stating that communications have been received from the Consul stating that the telegraph-line at Fang-k'ou has been destroyed by a mob consisting of soldiers dressed as common people who also attacked two Danes. The Board of Trade doubt that this can be true and furthermore the Board of Trade has constantly warned the Great Northern Telegraph Company about the resistance of the common people towards telegraphs.
= 2035 Konsulatsarkiver. Shanghai. Korrespondancesager m.v. 1842-94: Pakke 9, nr. 47.

126.

Date: 17 February (1875) - (Kuang-hsü 1), 1, 12.
From: W.S. Young, Vice-Consul of Denmark, Fuchou.
To: P'an Chün-chang, Fuchou.
Copy of a communication stating that on account of trouble with a local military force, the Board of Trade is requested to place an escort of thirty armed men for protection of the transport of the telegraph-equipment from Fang-k'ou to Fuchou. The officials are obliged to do so according to article 18 of the Treaty between Denmark and China.
= 2035 Konsulatsarkiver. Shanghai. Korrespondancesager m.v. 1842-94: Pakke 6, nr. 13.

127.

Date: 18 February (1875) - (Kuang-hsü 1), 1, 13.
From: Board of Trade, Fuchou.
To: Consul of Denmark, Fuchou.
Letter stating that an officer has been sent to Fang-k'ou to determine if it is necessary to protect the transport of the telegraph-equipment belonging to the Great Northern Telegraph Company from Fang-k'ou to Fuchou. Furthermore more information concerning the route is indispensable.
= 2035 Konsulatsarkiver. Shanghai. Korrespondancesager m.v. 1842-94: Pakke 9, nr. 54.

128.

Date: 25 February 1875 - (Kuang-hsü 1), 1, 20.
From: Board of Trade, Fuchou.
To: Consul of Denmark, Fuchou.
Copy of a letter stating that the Consul should press the Great Northern Telegraph Company to fix a day on which the transport of their telegraph-equipment from Fang-k'ou to Fuchou will take place, in order to facilitate protection of the transport by soldiers.
= 2035 Konsulatsarkiver. Shanghai. Korrespondancesager m.v. 1842-94: Pakke 6, nr. 14.

129.

Date: 26 February 1875 - (Kuang-hsü 1), 1, 21.
From: Board of Trade, Fuchou.
To: Consul of Denmark, Fuchou.
Copy of a letter in reply stating that as the Great Northern Telegraph company has fixed the date for the transport of their telegraph-equipment at the 27th of February, an official has been deputed as escort. It will not be necessary to call out soldiers as was previously intended.
= 2035 Konsulatsarkiver. Shanghai. Korrespondancesager m.v. 1842-94: Pakke 6, nr. 15.

130.

Date: 27 February 1875.
From: Board of Trade, Fuchou.
To: W.S. Young, Vice-Consul of Denmark, Fuchou.
Letter stating that missionaries should obtain permission from the Chinese authorities to preach and build churches in the interior of China through the Consuls of their countries.
= 2035 Konsulatsarkiver. Shanghai. Korrespondancesager m.v. 1842-94: Pakke 9, nr. 83.

131.

Date: 1 March 1875.
From: Harton, Consul of Denmark, Fuchou.
To: Board of Trade, Fuchou.
Copy of a communication stating that a strong escort of soldiers should accompany the transport of telegraph-equipment. The telegraph-line has recently been destroyed and the country is not pacified sufficiently for the employees of the Great Northern Telegraph Company to travel safely in the area.
= 2035 Konsulatsarkiver. Shanghai. Korrespondancesager m.v. 1842-94: Pakke 6, nr. 16.

132.

Date: 3 March 1875.
From: Board of Trade, Fuchou.
To: Consul of Denmark, Fuchou.
Letter stating that if the Great Northern Telegraph Company does not proceed with the transport of their telegraph-equipment immediately, the transport will not be protected at all.
= 2035 Konsulatsarkiver. Shanghai. Korrespondancesager m.v. 1842-94: Pakke 9, nr. 56.

133.

Date: 10 March 1875 - (Kuang-hsü 1), 2, 3.
From: P'an Chün-chang, Fuchou.
To: Consul of Denmark, Fuchou.
Copy of a letter stating that the telegraph-equipment owned by the Great Northern Telegraph Company has been brought to Fang-k'ou despite the protests of the common people and the warnings from the Chinese officials. However, a group of soldiers has been sent to Fang-k'ou to protect the transport to Fuchou. The Consul is requested to avoid further delays in this matter.
= 2035 Konsulatsarkiver. Shanghai. Korrespondancesager m.v. 1842-94: Pakke 6, nr. 17.

134.

Date: 16 March 1875 - (Kuang-hsü 1), 2, 9.
From: Board of Trade, Fuchou.
To: Consul of Denmark, Fuchou.
Copy of a letter in reply stating that the deeds for the property purchased by the Great Northern Telegraph Company will be officially stamped as soon as the questions about the graveyard have been settled. The local authorities have been instructed to protect the telegraph-line according to the decision of the Tsungli Yamen. In addition, the deputy officer has returned from Fang-k'ou because the Great Northern Telegraph Company did not proceed with the transport at the scheduled time.
= 2035 Konsulatsarkiver. Shanghai. Korrespondancesager m.v. 1842-94: Pakke 6, nr. 19.

135.

Date: (3 April 1875) - (Kuang-hsü 1), 2, 28.
From: Ting Chia-wei, Fuchou.
To: W.S. Young, Vice-Consul of Denmark, Fuchou.
Letter inviting the Danish interpreter Schultz to visit the Board of Trade on the 4th of April.
= 2035 Konsulatsarkiver. Shanghai. Korrespondancesager m.v. 1842-94: Pakke 9, nr. 57.

136.

Date: 11 April 1875 - (Kuang-hsü 1), 3, 6.
From: Board of Trade, Fuchou.
To: Consul of Denmark, Fuchou.
Copy of a letter in reply stating that Shen Pao-chen has not finished the affairs concerning the protection of Taiwan. Therefore the Danish interpreter Schultz should negotiate with an official from the Board of Trade, whereupon both will be sailed to Taiwan for a personal conference with Shen Pao-chen.
= 2035 Konsulatsarkiver. Shanghai. Korrespondancesager m.v. 1842-94: Pakke 6, nr. 20.

137.

Date: (12 April 1875) - Kuang-hsü 1, 3, 7.
From: Li Ho-nien, Governor-General + Wen-Yü, Commander-
      in-Chief + Wang K'ai-t'ai, Governor, Fuchou.
Copy of instructions stating that a letter has been received from the Tsungli Yamen instructing the Provincials to negotiate with the Great Northern Telegraph Company on a peaceful settlement of the disturbances in connection with the construction of the Fuchou-Amoy telegraph-line. Ting Chia-wei, the Prefect, has been instructed to negotiate with the Company.
Appended: A copy of the letter from the Tsungli Yamen.
= Store Nordiske Arkiv: Stationskasse. Foochow-Amoy Landlinier.

138.

Date: (21 May 1875) - Kuang-hsü 1, 4, -.
From: Ting Chia-wei, Inspector at the Board of Trade, Fuchou.
To: H. Dreyer, Director of the Great Northern Telegraph Company, Shanghai + W.S. Young, Vice-Consul of Denmark, Fuchou + M.M. DeLano, Consul of the United States of America, Fuchou.
Copy of a letter containing the agreement between the Great Northern Telegraph Company and the Chinese authorities concerning the purchase of the Fuchou-Amoy telegraph-line and the payment of an indemnity.
= Store Nordiske Arkiv: Overenskomster. Kina.

139.

Date: (8 June 1875) - Kuang-hsü 1, 5, 5.
From: Waldemar Rudolf Raasløff, Ambassador of Denmark, Shanghai.
To: Tsungli Yamen, Peking.
Copy of a communication notifying the Tsungli Yamen of the appointment of the Consul of Denmark at Fuchou, W.S. Young.
= 2035 Konsulatsarkiver. Shanghai. Korrespondancesager m.v. 1842-94: Pakke 9, nr. 60.

140.

Date:(12 June 1875) - (Kuang-hsü 1), 5, 9.
From: Szu-T'u Hsü, Fuchou.
To: W.S. Young, Vice-Consul of Denmark, Fuchou.
Letter notifying the Consul that Szu-T'u Hsü has been appointed Intendant of Customs in place of P'an Chün-chang, for whom it was very inconvenient to hold this post in addition to his usual duties.
= 2035 Konsulatsarkiver. Shanghai. Korrespondancesager m.v. 1842-94: Pakke 6, nr. 21.

141.

Date: (16 June 1875) - Kuang-hsü 1, 5, 13.
From: Tsungli Yamen, Peking.
To: Waldemar Rudolf Raasløff, Ambassador of Denmark, Shanghai.
Communication acknowledging the appointment of the Consul of Denmark at Fuchou, W.S. Young.
= 2035 Konsulatsarkiver. Shanghai. Korrespondancesager m.v. 1842-94: Pakke 9, nr. 38.

142.

Date: (1 July 1875) - Kuang-hsü 1, 5, 28.
From: Ku, Acting Military Intendant, Swatow.
To: Hinrick Andreas Dircks, Consul of Denmark, Swatow.
Communication stating that according to orders issued by
the Tsungli Yamen on the request of the Danish Envoy to
China, Waldemar Rudolf Raasløff, the Chinese authorities
should protect the telegraph-lines constructed in China.
Consequently the Intendant has issued proclamations
prohibiting theft and damage of telegraph-material.
= 2120 Konsulatsarkiver. Swatow, Indkomne breve 1894-1912:
nr. 19.

143.

Date: (12 July 1875) - (Kuang-hsü 1), 6, 10.
From: Consul of Denmark, Fuchou.
To: Board of Trade, Fuchou.
Copy of a communication stating that three Danes,
employed by the Great Northern Telegraph Company, have
been attacked at Fang-k'ou. It is requested that the
incident be investigated and the criminals prosecuted.
= 2035 Konsulatsarkiver. Shanghai. Korrespondancesager
m.v. 1842-94: Pakke 9, nr. 46.

144.

Date: 16 July (1875) - (Kuang-hsü 1), 6, 14.
From: Board of Trade, Fuchou.
To: W.S. Young, Consul of Denmark, Fuchou.
Letter in reply stating that a Chinese official has been
ordered to investigate the robbery of telegraph-equipment
from Henningsen, an employee of the Great Northern
Telegraph Company. His housekeeper, Huang Jui-ch'ui, and
his gatekeeper, Lin Tsun-po, have been transferred to
Fuchou to be questioned by a Judge.
= 2035 Konsulatsarkiver. Shanghai. Korrespondancesager
m.v. 1842-94: Pakke 9, nr. 73.

145.

Date: (28 July 1875) - Kuang-hsü (1), 6, 26.
From: Consul of Denmark, Fuchou.
To: Board of Trade, Fuchou.
Copy of a communication stating that an assault has been
made on a Danish subject, C.C. Bojesen, at Fang-k'ou when
a mob was trying to destroy the telegraph-equipment
stored there. Request is made that the criminals be
arrested and brought to trial.
= 2035 Konsulatsarkiver. Shanghai. Korrespondancesager
m.v. 1842-94: Pakke 8, nr. 2.

146.

Date: (31 July 1875) - (Kuang-hsü 1), 6, 29.
From: Szu-T'u Hsü, Fuchou.
To: W.S. Young, Consul of Denmark, Fuchou.
Letter stating that a report has been received concerning the case of two Danes employed by the Great Northern Telegraph Company who were attacked by local people at Fang-k'ou. The Chinese official who escorted the Danes has found no evidence of any violence. Consequently, the Magistrate cannot give orders to the local officials to prosecute the trouble-makers.
= 2035 Konsulatsarkiver. Shanghai. Korrespondancesager m.v. 1842-94: Pakke 6, nr. 22.

147.

Date: 2 August 1875.
From: W.S. Young, Consul of Denmark, Fuchou.
To: Board of Trade, Fuchou.
Copy of a communication stating that the Chinese authorities should use official communications in all cases relevant to the affairs of the Danish Consulate from now on.
= 2035 Konsulatsarkiver. Shanghai. Korrespondancesager m.v. 1842-94: Pakke 9, nr. 37.

148.

Date: 6 August 1875 - (Kuang-hsü 1), 7, 6.
From: Szu-T'u Hsü, Fuchou.
To: W.S. Young, Consul of Denmark, Fuchou.
Letter in reply stating that according to the decision of the Tsungli Yamen, unofficial letters should be used in the correspondence with Consuls who are merchants, as has been done hitherto.
= 2035 Konsulatsarkiver. Shanghai. Korrespondancesager m.v. 1842-94: Pakke 9, nr. 64.

149.

Copy of letter no. 148.
= 2035 Konsulatsarkiver. Shanghai. Korrespondancesager m.v. 1842-94: Pakke 6, nr. 23.

150.

Date: (12 August 1875) - (Kuang-hsü 1), 7, 12.
From: Board of Trade, Fuchou.
To: W.S. Young, Consul of Denmark, Fuchou.
Letter stating that official stamps have been affixed to the deeds for the property bought by the Great Northern Telegraph Company. They are hereby forwarded.
= 2035 Konsulatsarkiver. Shanghai. Korrespondancesager m.v. 1842-94: Pakke 9, nr. 43.

151.

Date: (26 August 1875) - Kuang-hsü 1, 7, 26.
Copy of an agreement signed the 4th of October 1875
between the Great Northern Telegraph Company and the
Chinese authorities concerning the lease of the Pagoda-
line from Nan-t'ai to Ma-wei to the Company to manage
for the Chinese until the 31st of December 1875.
= Store Nordiske Arkiv: Stationskasse. Foochow-Amoy
Landlinier.

152.

Date: (26 August 1875) - Kuang-hsü 1, 7, 26.
Copy of an agreement signed the 4th of October 1875
between the Great Northern Telegraph Company and the
Chinese authorities concerning the transfer of the Pagoda-
line from Nan-t'ai to Ma-wei in the vicinity of Fuchou to
become Chinese property.
= Store Nordiske Arkiv: Stationskasse. Foochow-Amoy
Landlinier.

153.

Date: 1 September 1875 - (Kuang-hsü 1), 8, 2.
From: Lin Ch'ing-yi, Fuchou.
To: W.S. Young, Consul of Denmark, Fuchou.
Letter stating that the three sedanchair-bearers that
were employed by Henningsen, an employee of the Great
Northern Telegraph Company, and who are accused of theft,
have been brought to Fuohou and will presently be brought
to trial at the Magistrate's Office.
= 2035 Konsulatsarkiver. Shanghai. Korrespondancesager
m.v. 1842-94: Pakke 6, nr. 24.

154.

Date: (21 September 1875) - (Kuang-hsü 1), 8, 22.
From: Board of Trade, Fuchou.
To: W.S. Young, Consul of Denmark, Fuchou.
Letter stating that it has been decided that the
Magistrate Cheng Szu-chien was falsely accused of
stealing the graveyard he sold to the Great Northern
Telegraph Company, as the site was not in the legal
possession of any individual. However, as a penalty
for selling a graveyard he must pay for the repairs on
the graves.
= 2035 Konsulatsarkiver. Shanghai. Korrespondancesager
m.v. 1842-94: Pakke 9, nr. 49.

155.

Date: 25 September 1875 - (Kuang-hsü 1), 8, 26.
From: Szu-T'u Hsü, Fuchou.
To: W.S. Young, Consul of Denmark, Fuchou.
Letter stating that according to the decision of the
Tsungli Yamen, Chinese merchants employed by foreign
business firms are not allowed to communicate with the
Chinese authorities through a foreign Consul. They
should present themselves directly to the Chinese
authorities.
= 2035 Konsulatsarkiver. Shanghai. Korrespondancesager
m.v. 1842-94: Pakke 6, nr. 25.

156.

Date: (31 October 1875) - (Kuang-hsü 1), 10, 3.
From: Szu-T'u Hsü, Fuchou.
To: W.S. Young, Consul of Denmark, Fuchou.
Letter stating that orders have been received from the
Governor of the Province providing that a Magistrate
from the Board of Trade and the Provincial Judge should
examine the case of the destructions on the Fuchou-Amoy
telegraph-line in order to avoid further disturbances.
= 2035 Konsulatsarkiver. Shanghai. Korrespondancesager
m.v. 1842-94: Pakke 6, nr. 26.

157.

Date: (7 November 1875) - Kuang-hsü 1, 10, 11.
From: Chang, Military Intendant, Swatow.
To: Hinrich Andreas Dircks, Consul of Denmark, Swatow.
Communication stating that according to a communication
from the Danish Consul, the proclamations prohibiting
theft of telegraph-equipment supposedly issued by the
previous Intendant have in fact never been posted in the
districts. Accordingly, orders have been issued to the
local authorities to put up the proclamations immediately.
= 2120 Konsulatsarkiver. Swatow. Indkomne breve 1894-1912:
nr. 20.

158.

Date: (20 November 1875).
From: Li Ho-nien, Governor-General, Fuchou.
To: W.S. Young, Consul of Denmark, Fuchou.
Letter in reply stating that Li Ho-nien is presently
occupied by the military examinations. Thus the visit of
the Danish Envoy, Waldemar Rudolf Raasløff, must be postponed.
= 2035 Konsulatsarkiver. Shanghai. Korrespondancesager
m.v. 1842-94: Pakke 9, nr. 61.

159.

Date: (21 November 1875) - Kuang-hsü 1, 10, 24.
From: Wen-Yü, Commander-in-chief, Fuchou.
To: W.S. Young, Consul of Denmark, Fuchou.
Order in reply approving of the decision of the Danish Envoy, Waldemar Rudolf Raasløff, to visit Wen-yü on the 22nd of November.
= 2035 Konsulatsarkiver. Shanghai. Korrespondancesager m.v. 1842-94: Pakke 9, nr. 50.

160.

Date: (21 November 1875) - (Kuang-hsü 1), 10, 24.
From: Szu-T'u Hsü, Fuchou.
To: W.S. Young, Consul of Denmark, Fuchou.
Letter stating that the visit of the Danish Envoy, Waldemar Rudolf Raasløff, must be postponed on account of the death of the Governor of Fukien and because the Governor-General is occupied by military examinations. In the meantime, Raasløff should have a conference with the Magistrate, P'an Chün-chang.
= 2035 Konsulatsarkiver. Shanghai. Korrespondancesager m.v. 1842-94: Pakke 9, nr. 72.

161.

Date: (22 November 1875) - (Kuang-hsü 1), 10, 25.
From: Szu-T'u Hsü, Fuchou.
To: Consul of Denmark, Fuchou.
Letter stating that Szu T'u Hsü will pay a visit to the Danish Envoy, Waldemar Rudolf Raasløff, on the 23rd of November.
= 2035 Konsulatsarkiver. Shanghai. Korrespondancesager m.v. 1842-94: Pakke 9, nr. 55.

162.

Date: 24 November 1875.
From: Li Ho-nien, Governor-General, Fuchou.
To: W.S. Young, Consul of Denmark, Fuchou.
Letter stating that Li Ho-nien has finished hearing the military examinations. Accordingly, a date can now be fixed for the visit of the Danish Envoy, Waldemar Rudolf Raasløff.
= 2035 Konsulatsarkiver. Shanghai. Korrespondancesager m.v.: Pakke 9, nr. 75.

163.

Date: (13 December 1875) - Kuang-hsu 1, 11, 16.
From: Henningsen, Agent of the Great Northern Telegraph
    Company, Fuchou.
To: Board of Trade, Fuchou.
Copy of a petition stating that unless the expenditures
of the Great Northern Telegraph Company for the repairs
on the destroyed parts of the Fuchou-Amoy telegraph-line
are paid within three days, the Company will withdraw
their employees and will not repair any damages that
might occur in the future.
Appended: Accounts for the expenditures.
= 2035 Konsulatsarkiver. Shanghai. Korrespondancesager
m.v. 1842-94: Pakke 6, nr. 27.

164.

Date: (16 December 1875) - (Kuang-hsu 1), 11, 19.
From: Board of Trade, Fuchou.
To: W.S. Young, Consul of Denmark, Fuchou.
Letter stating that instructions have been received from
the Governor-General stating that the inconsiderate
administration of the Magistrate, Chou Hsing-yi, has
created the disagreements between the Great Northern
Telegraph Company and the Chinese authorities. However,
it is the opinion of the Board of Trade that the Company
is solely responsible for the trouble and therefore Chou
Hsing-yi has been instructed to proceed with the removal
of the telegraph-line.
= 2035 Konsulatsarkiver. Shanghai. Korrespondancesager
m.v. 1842-94: Pakke 6, nr. 28.

165.

Date: (21 December 1875) - (Kuang-hsu 1), 11, 24.
From: Pao-Heng, Governor, Fuchou.
To: M.M. DeLano, Acting Consul of Denmark, Fuchou.
Letter stating that the difficulties created by the
resistance of the common people in an area south of
Fuchou has prevented the construction of the telegraph-
line. Furthermore, it is proposed that a sea-cable should
be constructed instead of a land-cable on the section
covered by the Fuchou-Amoy telegraph-line. It is earnestly
requested that the Consul will negotiate with the Great
Northern Telegraph Company for a satisfactory solution.
= 2035 Konsulatsarkiver. Shanghai. Korrespondancesager
m.v. 1842-94: Pakke 6, nr. 29.

166.

Date: (22 December 1875) - Kuang-hsü 1, 11, 25.
From: Board of Trade, Fuchou.
To: M.M. DeLano, Acting Consul of Denmark, Fuchou.
Communication in reply stating that the Board of Trade has received the communication from the Consul concerning the accounts of the Great Northern Telegraph Company for the repairs on the Fuchou-Amoy telegraph-line. A reply has been sent to Henningsen.
= 2035 Konsulatsarkiver. Shanghai. Korrespondancesager m.v. 1842-94: Pakke 6, nr. 31.

167.

Date: (23 December 1875) - Kuang-hsü 1, 11, 26.
From: Li Ho-nien, Governor-General, Fuchou.
To: M.M. DeLano, Acting Consul of Denmark, Fuchou.
Order in reply acknowledging the receipt of a petition from Henningsen stating that the employees of the Great Northern Telegraph Company have been withdrawn because the Chinese authorities have not paid the expenditures for the repairs on the line. Furthermore stating that a proclamation issued by the authorities has been treated with much contempt by a local District Magistrate. Consequently an official has been ordered to examine the case.
= 2035 Konsulatsarkiver. Shanghai. Korrespondancesager m.v. 1842-94: Pakke 6, nr. 30.

168.

Date: (28 December 1875) - Kuang-hsü 1, 12, 1.
From: Chang Meng-yüan, Acting Prefect, Fuchou.
To: M.M. DeLano, Acting Consul of Denmark, Fuchou.
Communication notifying the Consul of the appointment of Chang Meng-yüan as Intendant of Trade in place of Ting Chia-wei who has retired.
= 2035 Konsulatsarkiver. Shanghai. Korrespondancesager m.v. 1842-94: Pakke 6, nr. 32.

169.

Date: 17 February 1876 - (Kuang-hsü 2), 1, 23.
From: Szu-T'u Hsü, Fuchou.
To: W.S. Young, Consul of Denmark, Fuchou.
Letter in reply stating that the Chinese officials at the Board of Trade will visit the Inspector of the Great Northern Telegraph Company, Helland, to discuss the purchase of the Fuchou-Amoy telegraph-line by the Chinese authorities.
= 2035 Konsulatsarkiver. Shanghai. Korrespondancesager m.v. 1842-94: Pakke 9, nr. 36.

170.

Date: 29 February 1876 - (Kuang-hsü 2), 2, 5.
From: Szu-T'u Hsü, Fuchou.
To: W.S. Young, Consul of Denmark, Fuchou.
Letter stating that the proclamations concerning the Fuchou-Amoy telegraph-line have already been posted everywhere in the districts. If the officials of the Great Northern Telegraph Company have not seen it posted at Chin-chiang it is their own fault.
= 2035 Konsulatsarkiver. Shanghai. Korrespondancesager m.v. 1842-94: Pakke 9, nr. 74.

171.

Date: (12 March 1876) - Kuang-hsü 2, 2, 17.
From: Board of Trade, Fuchou.
To: W.S. Young, Consul of Denmark, Fuchou.
Communication stating the conditions of the Chinese authorities for the purchase of the Fuchou-Amoy telegraph-line from the Great Northern Telegraph Company.
= 2035 Konsulatsarkiver. Shanghai. Korrespondancesager m.v. 1842-94: Pakke 9, nr. 15.

172.

Date: 22 March 1876 - Kuang-hsü 2, 2, 27.
From: Board of Trade, Fuchou.
To: W.S. Young, Consul of Denmark, Fuchou.
Communication stating that on the 20th of March an agreement has been signed by the Chinese authorities and the Great Northern Telegraph Company concerning the purchase of the Fuchou-Amoy telegraph-line by the Chinese authorities. The previous agreement signed on the 21st of May 1875 is hereby cancelled.
Appended: A copy of the agreement of 20th March 1876.
= 2035 Konsulatsarkiver. Shanghai. Korrespondancesager m.v. 1842-94: Pakke 6, nr. 33.

173.

Date: 22 March 1876 - Kuang-hsü 2, 2, 27.
From: Board of Trade, Fuchou.
To: W.S. Young, Consul of Denmark, Fuchou.
Communication stating that on the 20th of March an agreement has been signed by the Chinese authorities and the Great Northern Telegraph Company concerning the establishment of a telegraph-school at Fuchou for Chinese students.
Appended: A copy of the agreement concerning the telegraph school.
= 2035 Konsulatsarkiver. Shanghai. Korrespondancesager m.v. 1842-94: Pakke 6, nr. 34.

174.

Date: (26 March 1876) - Kuang-hsü 2, 3, 1.
From: Board of Trade, Fuchou.
To: W.S. Young, Consul of Denmark, Fuchou.
Communication stating that a communication in reply has been received from the Consul stating that a copy of the agreement concerning the telegraph-school at Fuchou was not appended to the communication sent to the Consul of Denmark. Therefore a copy is included in this communication.
= 2035 Konsulatsarkiver. Shanghai. Korrespondancesager m.v. 1842-94: Pakke 6, nr. 35.

175.

Date: 15 September 1876 - Kuang-hsü 2, 7, -.
From: Chu Sung-shan.
To: Consul of Denmark.
Petition complaining that the Danish subject, Kofoed, has not paid the money he owes to Chu Sung-shan for planting trees. Furthermore, Kofoed had assaulted Chu Sung-shan physically when he came to beg for the money.
Appended: The bill for the trees planted.
= 2035 Konsulatsarkiver. Shanghai. Korrespondancesager m.v. 1842-94: Pakke 6, nr. 36.

176.

Date: 25 March 1877 - Kuang-hsü 3, 2, 11.
From: Board of Trade, Fuchou.
To: M.M. DeLano, Acting Consul of Denmark, Fuchou.
Communication stating that notice should be given in advance to the Chinese authorities when foreign warships are surveying along the coast of China and when foreigners are travelling in the interior.
= 2035 Konsulatsarkiver. Shanghai. Korrespondancesager m.v. 1842-94: Pakke 9, nr. 62.

177.

Date: (3 April 1879) - Kuang-hsü 5, 3, 12.
From: Chang, Assistant Inspector, Swatow.
To: Consul of Denmark, Swatow.
Copy of a communication stating that a complaint has been received from the Foreign Consuls stating that the fishing-rods of the local Chinese fishermen are obstructing the free passage of ships on their way in and out of the port. Accordingly, the provincial authorities have commissioned the Expectant Magistrate T'ien Chih-hsüan to examine the problem together with the Intendant.
= 2120 Konsulatsarkiver. Swatow. Indkomne breve 1894-1912.

178.

Date: 17 May 1880 - Kuang-hsü 6, 4, 9.
From: P'u-An, Colonel, Nan-t'ai.
To: Walter Allum, Consul of Denmark, Fuchou.
Communication notifying the Consul of the appointment of P'u-An as Intendant of Customs at Nan-t'ai.
= 1039 Konsulatsarkiver. Foochow, Indkomne breve m.m. 1862-93: nr. 43.

179.

Date: (11 January 1881) - Kuang-hsü 6, 12, 12.
From: P'eng Ao.
To: Consul of Russia.
Letter stating that the Chinese authorities will draw up a legal settlement in the case against the foreign business firm "Fu-ch'ang" concerning lease of a property.
= 2035 Konsulatsarkiver. Shanghai. Korrespondancesager m.v. 1842-94: Pakke 7, nr. 1.

180.

Date: 7 June 1881 - Kuang-hsü 7, 5, -.
From: Henningsen, Agent of the Great Northern Telegraph Company, Shanghai.
To: Li Hung-chang, Superintendant of Trade at the Northern Ports, Tientsin.
Copy of a petition requesting that an agreement of 6 articles be concluded between the Great Northern Telegraph Company and the Chinese Government. The agreement provides that the Company will have a monopoly on construction of telegraph-lines in China for 20 years. In return, all official telegrams to or from the High Authorities in China will be transmitted by the lines owned by the Great Northern Telegraph Company without any charge.
= Store Nordiske Arkiv: Gl. Dokumentkasse, Concessioner og Overenskomster. Kina.

181.

Date: 1 July 1881 - (Kuang-hsü 7, 6), 12.
From: Li Hung-chang, Superintendant of Trade at the Northern Ports, Tientsin.
To: L. Waeber, Acting Consul of Denmark, Tientsin.
Copy of an endorsement stating that the agreement of 6 articles proposed by the Agent of the Great Northern Telegraph Company, Henningsen, in a petition is hereby acknowledged. Instructions have been issued to act in accordance with the proposal.
= Store Nordiske Arkiv: Gl. Dokumentkasse, Concessioner og Overenskomster. Kina.

182.

Date: (15 December 1882) - Kuang-hsü 8, 11, 6.
From: Yeh Yung-yüan, Fuchou.
To: Walter Allum, Consul of Denmark, Fuchou.
Letter stating that Yeh Yung-yüan has returned from a journey to the capital.
= 1039 Konsulatsarkiver. Foochow. Indkomne breve m.m. 1862-93: nr. 42.

183.

Date: 1883.
From: Ho Ching, Governor-General, Fuchou.
Copy of a letter of comment stating that the Great Northern Telegraph Company cannot be allowed to build an additional telegraph-line in Fukien, because the cables are regarded as dangerous according to the theories of Fengshui, and thus likely to cause trouble with the common people.
= 1039 Konsulatsarkiver. Foochow. Indkomne breve m.m. 1862-93: nr. 41.

184.

Date: (27 January 1883) - Kuang-hsü 8, 12, 19.
From: Ch'eng Ts'un, Colonel, Nan-t'ai.
To: Walter Allum, Consul of Denmark, Fuchou.
Communication notifying the Consul of the appointment of Ch'eng-Ts'un as Intendant of Customs at Nan-t'ai.
= 1039 Konsulatsarkiver. Foochow. Indkomne breve m.m. 1862-93: nr. 41.

185.

Date: (6 November 1883) - Kuang-hsü 9, 10, 7.
From: British Consul, Taiwan.
To: Chou, Magistrate, Swatow.
Copy of a letter stating that a petition has been received from the owner of the British business firm "Yi-ho", stating that on account of the liquidation of the comprador of the firm, Chang Yi-hsin, the Magistrate is requested to call his companion, Hsiao T'ien, to the court as a witness.
= 2120 Konsulatsarkiver. Swatow. Indkomne breve 1894-1912: nr. 23.

186.

Date: 8 April 1885 - Kuang-hsü 11, 2, 23.
From: Consul of Denmark, Swatow.
To: Chu, Expectant Magistrate, Swatow.
Communication notifying the Magistrate of the appointment of the Danish Consul.
= 2120 Konsulatsarkiver. Swatow. Indkomne breve 1894-1912: nr. 12.

187.

Date: 8 April 1885 - Kuang-hsü 11, 2, 23.
From: Consul of Denmark, Swatow.
To: Hsu-T'ung, Acting Sub-Prefect, Swatow.
Communication notifying the Sub-Prefect of the appointment of the Danish Consul.
= 2120 Konsulatsarkiver. Swatow. Indkomne breve 1894-1912: nr. 13.

188.

Date: (29 April 1885) - Kuang-hsü 11, 3, 16.
From: Chang, Military Intendant, Swatow.
To: Consul of Denmark, Swatow.
Communication acknowledging the appointment of the Danish Consul in lieu of Robert Craig.
= 2120 Konsulatsarkiver. Swatow. Indkomne breve 1894-1912: nr. 14.

189.

Date: 7 October (1886) - Kuang-hsü 12, 9, 10.
From: T'ieh, Expectant Sub-Prefect, Swatow.
To: Walter Allum, Consul of Denmark, Swatow.
Communication notifying the Consul of the appointment of T'ieh as Commissioner of Customs.
= 2120 Konsulatsarkiver. Swatow. Indkomne breve 1894-1912: nr. 10.

190.

Date: 29 November 1887 - Kuang-hsü 13, 10, 15.
From: Hsia, Expectant Magistrate, Swatow.
To: E.F. Alford, Consul of Denmark, Swatow.
Communication notifying the Consul of the appointment of Hsia as Commissioner of Customs at Ch'ao-chou (Swatow).
= 2120 Konsulatsarkiver. Swatow. Indkomne breve 1894-1912: nr. 7.

191.

Date: (1888).
From: Hsü-T'ung, Acting Sub-Prefect, Swatow.
To: British Consul, Taiwan.
Letter in reply stating that a communication has been received from the British Consul stating that a village constable has confiscated some bags onboard a ship from the "Yi-ho" business firm. The actual facts of the case are that the ship was detained for examination outside the port because the list of goods did not tally with the actual load on the ship.
= 2120 Konsulatsarkiver. Swatow. Indkomne breve 1894-1912: nr. 4.

192.

Date: 26 June 1888 - (Kuang-hsü 14), 5, 17.
From: Kung Chao-yüan, Military Intendant, Shanghai.
To: John MacGregor, Consul of Denmark, Shanghai.
Letter stating that on the request of the British Consul-General Hughes, the hours for practice with the guns at the forts along the river have been made public and are announced in the local newspapers. In addition, a red flag will be hoisted at the forts before the shooting commences.
= 2035 Konsulatsarkiver. Shanghai. Indkomne breve 1887-93: nr. 9.

193.

Date: 11 July 1888 - (Kuang-hsü 14), 6, 3.
From: Kung Chao-yüan, Military Intendant, Shanghai.
To: John MacGregor, Consul of Denmark, Shanghai.
Letter stating that on two occasions the American Mission has been granted exemption from the Likin-tax on some material for construction of houses that they transported into the interior of China. This, however, is not intended to serve as a precedent in the future.
= 2035 Konsulatsarkiver. Shanghai. Indkomne breve 1887-93: nr. 8.

194.

Date: (3 December 1888) - Kuang-hsü 14, 11, 1.
From: Hsü-T'ung, Acting Sub-Prefect, Swatow.
To: E.F. Alford, Consul of Denmark, Swatow.
Communication notifying the Consul of the appointment of Hsü-T'ung as Commissioner of Customs.
= 2120 Konsulatsarkiver. Swatow. Indkomne breve 1894-1912: nr. 9.

195.

Date: (9-15 March 1889) - (Kuang-hsü 15), 2, 8-14.
Copies of six letters exchanged between Liu, the Military Intendant and the Inspector of Customs at Tientsin and the Acting Consul of Denmark concerning 95 boxes with commodities imported by the Danish subject Kierulff for his shop in Peking. Mr. Kierulff wants duty-exemption for the commodities as they will be sold to the legations. The Chinese officials will only grant duty-exemption for commodities that are imported directly by the legations for their own use.
= 426 Gesandtskabsarkiver. Peking. 1891-1908: Kierulff.

196.

Date: (14 April 1889) - Kuang-hsü 13, 3, 21.
From: Te-T'ai, Military Intendant, Swatow.
To: E.F. Alford, Consul of Denmark, Swatow.
Letter in reply stating that the passport for the Danish subject who is employed by the Telegraph Company for a trip to Kwangtung province has been duly stamped and the local authorities of the said province have been informed.
= 2120 Konsulatsarkiver. Swatow. Indkomne breve 1894-1912: nr. 1.

197.

Date: (25 April - May 1889) - (Kuang-hsü 15), 3, 26 - 4, 7.
Copies of five letters exchanged between Liu, the Military Intendant and Inspector of Customs at Tientsin and the Acting Consul of Denmark at Tientsin concerning the commodities imported by the Danish merchant Kierulff. In addition a copy of a letter to Li Hung-chang stating that the Military Intendant of Tientsin refuses to grant exemption from duty for the commodities and requesting that Li Hung-chang will order the Customs to grant the exemption.
= 426 Gesandtskabsarkiver. Peking. 1891-1908: Kierulff.

198.

Date: (November 1889).
From: Chang Mei-ch'üan.
To: John MacGregor, Consul of Denmark, Shanghai.
Petition asking the Consul to persuade the Great Northern Telegraph Company to give Chang Mei-ch'üan the salary that the deceased Danish Subject, J.M. Holst, owed to him.
= 2035 Konsulatsarkiver. Shanghai. Korrespondancesager m.v. 1842-94: Pakke 7, nr. 2.

199.

Date: 18 November 1889 - Kuang-hsü 15, 10, -.
From: Li A-wen, Tailor, Shanghai.
To: John MacGregor, Consul of Denmark, Shanghai.
Petition asking the Consul to take care that Li A-wen gets the bill for the clothes bought by the Danish subject J.M. Holst, who has recently died, paid by the estate.
= 2035 Konsulatsarkiver. Shanghai. Korrespondancesager m.v. 1842-94: Pakke 7, nr. 3.

200.

Date: 21 November 1889 - Kuang-hsü 15, -, 29.
From: T'ieh, Expectant Sub-Prefect + Liu, Expectant
    Prefect, Swatow.
To: E.F. Alford, Consul of Denmark, Swatow.
Communication notifying the Consul of the appointment of T'ieh and Liu as Commissioners of Customs at Ch'ao-chou (Swatow).
= 2120 Konsulatsarkiver. Swatow. Indkomne breve 1894-1912: nr. 6.

201.

Date: (18 January 1890).
From: Yang Shih-ao, Expectant Prefect + En, Expectant
    Sub-Prefect, Swatow.
To: E.F. Alford, Consul of Denmark, Swatow.
Communication notifying the Consul of the appointment of Yang Shih-ao and En as Commissioners of Customs.
= 2120 Konsulatsarkiver. Swatow. Indkomne breve 1894-1912: nr. 17.

202.

Date: 26 March 1890 - (Kuang-hsü 16), Jun2, 6.
From: Kuang Chao-yüan, Military Intendant, Shanghai.
To: John MacGregor, Consul of Denmark, Shanghai.
Letter stating that in legal cases by a Chinese subject against a foreign subject, the Chinese authorities have decided to send an official from the Board of Foreign Affairs to sit in at the trial at the Consulate of the defendant's country.
= 2035 Konsulatsarkiver. Shanghai. Indkomne breve 1887-93: nr. 6.

203.

Date: 31 March 1890 - (Kuang-hsü 16), Jun2, 11.
From: Kung Chao-yüan, Military Intendant, Shanghai.
To: John MacGregor, Consul of Denmark, Shanghai.
Letter stating that the Chinese authorities approve of the proposition made by the Magistrate at the Mixed Court of Shanghai which is that the Chinese merchants should give sufficient security for their liquidity when they sign a contract with a foreign firm for delivery of imported goods.
= 2035 Konsulatsarkiver. Shanghai. Indkomne breve 1887-93: nr. 5.

204.

Date: (2 April 1890) - Kuang-hsü 16, Jun2, 13.
From: Sun To-hsin, Expectant Law-secretary, Swatow.
To: E.F. Alford, Consul of Denmark, Swatow.
Communication notifying the Consul of the appointment of Sun To-hsin as Commissioner of Customs in co-operation with Yang Shih-ao.
= 2120 Konsulatsarkiver. Swatow. Indkomne breve 1894-1912: nr. 8.

205.

Date: 9 April 1890 - (Kuang-hsü 16), Jun2, 20.
From: Kung Chao-yüan, Military Intendant, Shanghai.
To: John MacGregor, Consul of Denmark, Shanghai.
Letter stating that orders have been received from the Tsungli Yamen stating that on the request of the German Minister to Peking, Max von Brandt, the Chinese authorities are instructed to issue passports for missionaries travelling in the interior of China with the name in English as well as in Chinese.
= 2035 Konsulatsarkiver. Shanghai. Indkomne breve 1887-93: nr. 7.

206.

Date: 15 April 1890 - (Kuang-hsü 16), Jun2, 26.
From: Nieh Ch'i-kuei, Military Intendant, Shanghai.
To: John MacGregor, Consul of Denmark, Shanghai.
Letter notifying the Consul of the appointment of Nieh Ch'i-kuei as Military Intendant of Shanghai in lieu of Kung Chao-yüan.
= 2035 Konsulatsarkiver. Shanghai. Indkomne breve 1887-93: nr. 4.

207.

Date: (4 June 1891) - Kuang-hsü 17, 4, 28.
From: Yang Shih-ao, Expectant Prefect + Sun To-hsin,
    Expectant Law-Secretary, Swatow.
To: W.A. Cruickshank, Consul of Denmark, Swatow.
Communication acknowledging the appointment of the Danish Consul, W.A. Cruickshank, in lieu of E.F. Alford.
= 2120 Konsulatsarkiver. Swatow. Indkomne breve 1894-1912: nr. 16.

208.

Date: (7 June 1891) - Kuang-hsü 17, 5, 1.
From: Liang, Deputy, Swatow.
To: W.A. Cruickshank, Consul of Denmark, Swatow.
Communication acknowledging the appointment of the Danish Consul, W.A. Cruickshank, in lieu of E.F. Alford.
= 2120 Konsulatsarkiver. Swatow. Indkomne breve 1894-1912: nr. 21.

209.

Date: (17 June 1891) - Kuang-hsü 17, 5, 11.
From: Ku, Acting Military Intendant, Swatow.
To: W.A. Cruickshank, Consul of Denmark, Swatow.
Communication acknowledging the appointment of the Danish Consul, W.A. Cruickshank, in lieu of E.F. Alford.
= 2120 Konsulatsarkiver. Swatow. Indkomne breve 1894-1912: nr. 11.

210.

Date: (19 September 1891) - Kuang-hsü 17, 11, 17.
From: Sun To-hsin, Expectant Law-Secretary + Yang Shih-ao, Expectant Prefect, Swatow.
To: W.A. Cruickshank, Consul of Denmark, Swatow.
Communication notifying the Consul of the appointment of Sun To-hsin and Yang Shih-ao as Commissioners of Customs at Ch'ao-chou (Swatow).
= 2120 Konsulatsarkiver. Swatow. Indkomne breve 1894-1912: nr. 2.

211.

Date: (April 1892).
From: The Imperial Chinese Telegraph Company.
To: Herbert Smith, Consul of Denmark, Shanghai.
Letter stating that according to the contract between C.C. Bojesen, who has recently gone insane, and the Imperial Chinese Telegraph Company, the Company is to pay the fee for C.C. Bojesen's journey back to Denmark. Therefore the sum of 246 dollars is herewith forwarded.
= 2035 Konsulatsarkiver. Shanghai. Korrespondancesager m.v. 1842-94: Pakke 8, nr. 4.

212.

Date: (19 April 1892) - Kuang-hsü (18), 3, 23.
From: The Imperial Chinese Telegraph Company.
To: Herbert Smith, Consul of Denmark, Shanghai.
Letter stating that because the Danish subject C.C. Bojesen has gone insane while he was employed by the Chinese Telegraph Company, his contract with the Company is hereby cancelled. The Company forwards 200 dollars, the salary for the period 1-15 April.
= 2035 Konsulatsarkiver. Shanghai. Korrespondancesager m.v. 1842-94: Pakke 8, nr. 3.

213.

Date: 7 June 1892 - (Kuang-hsü 18), 5, 13.
From: Nieh Ch'i-kuei, Military Intendant, Shanghai.
To: John MacGregor, Consul of Denmark, Shanghai.
Communication acknowledging the appointment of John MacGregor as Consul of Denmark.
= 2035 Konsulatsarkiver. Shanghai. Indkomne breve 1887-93: nr. 3.

214.

Date: (17 September 1892) - Kuang-hsü 18, 8, 27.
From: Sun To-hsin, Expectant Law-Secretary + Yang
     Shih-ao, Expectant Prefect, Swatow.
To: David MacHaffie, Consul of Denmark, Swatow.
Communication acknowledging the appointment of the Danish Consul, David MacHaffie.
= 2120 Konsulatsarkiver. Swatow. Indkomne breve 1894-1912: nr. 5.

215.

Date: (18 September 1892) - Kuang-hsü 18, 8, 28.
From: Liang, Assistant Magistrate, Fuchou.
To: David MacHaffie, Consul of Denmark, Swatow.
Communication acknowledging the appointment of the Danish Consul, David MacHaffie, in lieu of W.A. Cruickshank.
= 2120 Konsulatsarkiver. Swatow. Indkomne breve 1894-1912: nr. 23.

216.

Date: 26 July 1893 - (Kuang-hsü 19), 6, 14.
From: Tsai, Magistrate, Shanghai.
To: John MacGregor, Consul of Denmark, Shanghai.
(Incomplete and mutilated) letter stating the facts of the case of Lu Tzu-tung against Wu Shan-miao, namely that a telegram from Singapore to Lu Tzu-tung's firm had been decoded with wrong characters at the telegraph office so that it was delivered at the firm of Wu Shan-miao, where it was mislaid. Therefore Lu Tzu-tung claims the payment of a loss of 400 taels.
= 2035 Konsulatsarkiver. Shanghai. Indkomne breve 1887-93: nr. 2.

217.

Date: (16 August 1893) - (Kuang-hsü 19), 8, 14.
From: Nieh Ch'i-kuai, Military Intendant, Shanghai.
To: Carl Alfred Bock, Consul of Denmark, Shanghai.
Letter acknowledging the appointment of the Consul-General of Sweden and Norway, Carl Alfred Bock, as Consul of Denmark.
= 2035 Konsulatsarkiver. Shanghai. Indkomne breve 1887-93: nr. 1.

218.

Date: 4 August 1894 - Kuang-hsü 20, 7, 4.
From: Ch'en Ming-chih, Military Intendant, Fuchou.
To: N.A. Popoff, Consul of Russia and Denmark, Fuchou.
Communication notifying N.A. Popoff of the circumstances of the outbreak of the Sino-Japanese War. Orders have been issued to destroy all Japanese ships entering the port of Fuchou.
= 1039 Konsulatsarkiver. Foochow. Indkomne breve m.m. 1862-93: nr. 3.

219.

Date: 4 August 1894 - Kuang-hsü 20, 7, 4.
From: Ch'eng Ming-chih, Military Intendant, Fuchou.
To: N.A. Popoff, Consul of Russia and Denmark, Fuchou.
Communication notifying the Consul that the entrance to the port will be mined on account of the Sino-Japanese War. Ships from foreign countries should give notice in advance to the Mining Battalion when approaching the port, so that they can be piloted into the harbour.
= 1039 Konsulatsarkiver. Foochow. Indkomne breve m.m. 1862-93: nr. 3.

220.

Date: 9 August 1894.
From: Ch'en Ming-chih, Military Intendant, Fuchou.
To: N.A. Popoff, Consul of Russia and Denmark, Fuchou.
Letter notifying the Consul that the port entrance was mined on the 8th of August. Ships should anchor outside the port and wait for the pilot to be sailed out to them in boats carrying a red flag during daytime and a lamp during the night.
= 1039 Konsulatsarkiver. Foochow. Indkomne breve m.m. 1862-93: nr. 5.

221.

Date: 29 August 1894 - Kuang-hsü 20, 7, 29.
From: Ch'en Ming-chih, Military Intendant, Fuchou.
To: N.A. Popoff, Consul of Russia and Denmark, Fuchou.
Communication stating that orders have been issued by the Tsungli Yamen, stating that all foreigners will be protected as usual in spite of the Sino-Japanese War. Appended: A copy of a communication to all foreign governments from the Tsungli Yamen stating the standpoints of the Chinese Government concerning the Sino-Japanese War.
= 1039 Konsulatsarkiver. Foochow. Indkomne breve m.m. 1862-93: nr. 6.

222.

Date: (30 August 1894) - Kuang-hsü 20, 7, 30.
From: Ch'en Ming-chih, Military Intendant, Fuchou.
To: N.A. Popoff, Consul of Russia and Denmark, Fuchou.
Communication notifying the Consul that merchant ships should anchor outside the port and be examined before being piloted into the harbour. The port has been mined on account of the Sino-Japanese War.
= 1039 Konsulatsarkiver. Foochow. Indkomne breve m.m. 1862-93: nr. 1.

223.

Date: 31 August 1894 - (Kuang-hsü 20), 8, 1.
From: Ch'en Ming-chih, Military Intendant, Fuchou.
To: N.A. Popoff, Consul of Russia and Denmark, Fuchou.
Letter notifying the Consul of the appointment of Ch'en Ming-chih as Acting Prefect of Fuchou and Ningpo. He will manage the trade affairs together with Ho.
= 1039 Konsulatsarkiver. Foochow. Indkomne breve m.m. 1862-93: nr. 7.

224.

Date: (6 September 1894) - Kuang-hsü 20, 8, 7.
From: Fang, Prefect, Fuchou.
To: N.A. Popoff, Consul of Russia and Denmark, Fuchou.
Communication requesting that the two Russian business firms, "Fu-ch'ang" and "Shun-feng", are ordered to pay their tax immediately.
= 1039 Konsulatsarkiver. Foochow. Indkomne breve m.m. 1862-93: nr. 2.

225.

Date: 1 October 1894 - Kuang-hsü 20, 9, (2).
From: Yang Wen-ting, Acting Military Intendant, Fuchou.
To: N.A. Popoff, Consul of Russia and Denmark, Fuchou.
Communication stating that the Chinese authorities have approved of the proposal of the Consul of Great Britain, namely that the Consuls should affix seals to the telegrams in secret language sent by merchants of their countries.
Appended: A copy of the regulations proposed by the British Consul.
= 1039 Konsulatsarkiver. Foochow. Indkomne breve m.m. 1862-93: nr. 8.

226.

Date: 8 October 1894 - Kuang-hsü 20, 9, 10.
From: T'an Chung-lin, Governor-General, Fuchou.
To: N.A. Popoff, Consul of Russia and Denmark, Fuchou.
Communication stating that on account of the blockade of the port of Fuchou, the merchant ships should anchor outside the port and their cargo should then be trans-shipped to the harbour.
= 1039 Konsulatsarkiver. Foochow. Indkomne breve m.m. 1862-93: nr. 9.

227.

Date: (24 December 1894) - Kuang-hsü 20, 11, 28.
From: Ch'en Ming-chih, Military Intendant, Fuchou.
To: N.A. Popoff, Consul of Russia and Denmark, Fuchou.
Communication notifying the Consul that Ch'en Ming-chih has returned to the post as Manager of Trade Affairs. Therefore the responsibilities of the affairs of the Commander-in-chief at Fuchou will be managed by the Governor-General.
= 1039 Konsulatsarkiver. Foochow. Indkomne breve m.m. 1862-93: nr. 11.

228.

Date: (31 December 1894) - Kuang-hsü 20, 12, 5.
From: Yang Wen-ting, Acting Military Intendant, Fuchou.
To: N.A. Popoff, Consul of Russia and Denmark, Fuchou.
Communication notifying the Consul that the merchant ships that have anchored outside the port should leave at once when the forts are fighting with Japanese ships. If possible, notice will be given in advance.
= 1039 Konsulatsarkiver. Foochow. Indkomne breve 1862-93: nr. 10.

229.

Date: 5 January 1895 - Kuang-hsü 20, 12, 10.
From: Ch'en Ming-chih, Military Intendant, Fuchou.
To: N.A. Popoff, Consul of Russia and Denmark, Fuchou.
Communication stating that orders have been issued by the Tsungli Yamen providing that all merchants who are not employed by the Chinese authorities must use plain language in their telegrams, while officials of all countries are allowed to use secret language.
= 1039 Konsulatsarkiver. Foochow. Indkomne breve m.m. 1862-93: nr. 12.

230.

Date: (11 January 1895) - (Kuang-hsü 20), 12, 16.
From: Ch'en Ming-chih, Military Intendant, Fuchou.
To: N.A. Popoff, Consul of Russia and Denmark, Fuchou.
Letter notifying the Consul of the appointment of Ho as Magistrate of the An-chi district. The responsibilities of the post of Inspector of the Board of Trade is hereby transferred to the Expectant Prefect, Chu.
= 1039 Konsulatsarkiver. Foochow. Indkomne breve m.m. 1862-93: nr. 13.

231.

Date: 2 February 1895 - (Kuang-hsü 21), 1, 8.
From: Ch'en Ming-chih, Military Intendant, Fuchou.
To: N.A. Popoff, Consul of Russia and Denmark, Fuchou.
Letter stating that foreigners who wish to travel in the neighbourhood of Fuchou, should give notice in advance to the Chinese authorities because the common people are afraid of Japanese spies.
= 1039 Konsulatsarkiver. Foochow. Indkomne breve m.m. 1862-93: nr. 14.

232.

Date: 27 April 1895 - Kuang-hsü 21, 4, 3.
From: Ch'en Ming-chih, Military Intendant, Fuchou.
To: N.A. Popoff, Consul of Russia and Denmark, Fuchou.
Communication notifying the Consul of the appointment of the Governor-General, Pien Shih-ch'üan. Pien Shih-ch'üan takes over the responsibilities of the post from T'an Chung-lin.
= 1039 Konsulatsarkiver. Foochow. Indkomne breve m.m. 1862-93: nr. 15.

233.

Date: 2 June 1895 - Kuang-hsü 21, 5, 10.
From: Ch'en Ming-chih, Military Intendant, Fuchou.
To: N.A. Popoff, Consul of Russia and Denmark, Fuchou.
Communication stating that the law providing that all telegrams in secret language must have the seals of the Consulate affixed has been abrogated.
= 1039 Konsulatsarkiver. Foochow. Indkomne breve m.m. 1862-93: nr. 16.

234.

Date: (2 July 1895) - Kuang-hsü 21, Jun5, 10.
From: Ch'in, Acting Prefect, Fuchou.
To: N.A. Popoff, Consul of Russia and Denmark, Fuchou.
Communication notifying the Consul of the appointment of
Ch'in as Associate Manager of Trade Affairs at Fuchou.
= 1034 Konsulatsarkiver. Foochow, Indkomne breve
m.m. 1862-93: nr. 17.

235.

Date: (18 August) 1895 - (Kuang-hsü 21), 6, 29.
From: Ch'en Ming-chih, Military Intendant, Fuchou.
To: N.A. Popoff, Consul of Russia and Denmark, Fuchou.
Letter notifying the Consul of the appointment of Nieh
Yüan-lung as Associate Inspector at the Board of Trade.
= 1039 Konsulatsarkiver. Foochow. Indkomne breve
m.m. 1862-93: nr. 18.

236.

Date: 1 September 1895 - Kuang-hsü 21, 7, 13.
From: Ch'en Ming-chih, Military Intendant + Hsü,
    Acting Military Intendant, Fuchou.
To: N.A. Popoff, Consul of Russia and Denmark, Fuchou.
Communication notifying the Consul of the appointment of
Hsü as Associate Manager of Trade Affairs at Fuchou.
= 1039 Konsulatsarkiver. Foochow. Indkomne breve
m.m. 1862-93: nr. 20.

237.

Date: 26 October 1895 - Kuang-hsü 21, 9, 9.
Notice to mariners no. 299 China Sea, Canton district.
Notifying the discovery of a rock on the north side of
the channel inside the "Lyeemoon".
(4 printed notices with text in English and Chinese).
= 2035 Konsulatsarkiver. Shanghai. Korrespondancesager
m.v. 1842-94: Pakke 8, nr. 1.

238.

Date: (2 January 1896) - Kuang-hsü 21, 11, 18.
From: Ch'en Ming-chih, Military Intendant + Hsü,
    Acting Military Intendant, Fuchou.
To: N.A. Popoff, Consul of Russia and Denmark, Fuchou.
Communication stating that foreign firms are not
permitted to use the designations of an office on the
caps of the messenger-runners.
= 1039 Konsulatsarkiver. Foochow. Indkomne breve
m.m. 1862-93: nr. 19.

239.

Date: 1 July 1896 - Kuang-hsü 22, 5, 21.
From: T'ang Pao-chien, Military Intendant, Fuchou.
To: N.A. Popoff, Consul of Russia and Denmark, Fuchou.
Communication notifying the Consul of the appointment of
T'ang Pao-chien as Manager of Trade Affairs at Fuchou.
= 1039 Konsulatsarkiver. Foochow. Indkomne breve
m.m. 1862-93: nr. 22.

240.

Date: 11 July 1896.
Agreement between China, the Great Northern Telegraph
Company and the Eastern Extension Telegraph Company on a
joint-purse budget for the incomes from telegram-fees for
telegrams to and from China.
= Store Nordiske Arkiv.

241.

Date: October 1896 - Kuang-hsü 22, 9, -.
From: Tun Ch'ang-tsai.
To: Consul of Russia, Fuchou.
Petition requesting the Consul of Russia to persuade the
Chinese authorities to re-examine the case of the illegal
opium-shop, so that the innocence of Tun Ch'ang-tsai may
be proved.
= 1039 Konsulatsarkiver. Foochow. Indkomne breve
m.m. 1862-93: nr. 21.

242.

Date: 13 November 1896 - Kuang-hsü 22, 10, 9.
From: T'ang Pao-chien, Military Intendant + Ch'en Ming-
      chih, Assistant Intendant, Fuchou.
To: N.A. Popoff, Consul of Russia and Denmark, Fuchou.
Communication notifying the Consul of the appointment of
T'ang Pao-chien and Ch'en Ming-chih as Managers of Trade
Affairs at Fuchou.
= 1039 Konsulatsarkiver. Foochow. Indkomne breve
m.m. 1862-93: nr. 23.

243.

Date: 22 November 1896 - Kuang-hsü 22, 10, 18.
From: Hu Ch'ang-t'u, Prefect, Fuchou.
To: N.A. Popoff, Consul of Russia and Denmark, Fuchou.
Communication notifying the Consul of the appointment
of Hu Ch'ang-t'u as Manager of Trade Affairs at Fuchou.
= 1039 Konsulatsarkiver. Foochow. Indkomne breve
m.m. 1862-93: nr. 24.

244.

Date: (9 December 1896) - Kuang-hsü 22, 11, 5.
From: T'ang Pao-chien, Military Intendant + Ch'en
    Ming-chih, Assistant Intendant, Fuchou.
To: N.A. Popoff, Consul of Russia and Denmark, Fuchou.
Communication stating that foreign steamers entering the
port and foreigners travelling along the coast should
give notice in advance in order to facilitate their
protection.
= 1039 Konsulatsarkiver. Foochow. Indkomne breve
m.m. 1862-93: nr. 25.

245.

Date: 14 February 1897 - Kuang-hsü 23, 1, 13.
From: T'ang Pao-chien, Military Intendant + Ch'en
    Ming-chih, Assistant Intendant + Nieh Yüan-lung,
    Expectant Intendant, Fuchou.
To: N.A. Popoff, Consul of Russia and Denmark, Fuchou.
Communication notifying the Consul of the appointment
of Nieh Yüan-lung as Assistant Manager of Trade Affairs
at Fuchou.
= 1039 Konsulatsarkiver. Foochow. Indkomne breve
m.m. 1862-93: nr. 26.

246.

Date: 13 May 1897.
Agreement between China and the Great Northern Telegraph
Company concerning a joint-purse budget for the incomes
from fees for telegrams transmitted between Russia and
China.
= Store Nordiske Arkiv.

247.

Date: 13 May 1897.

Declaration by China, the Great Northern Telegraph Company
and the Eastern Extension Telegraph Company stating that
the telegraph-cables to Nan-t'ai and Amoy should be
worked according to the Agreement of 11 July 1896.
= Store Nordiske Arkiv.

248.

Date: 20 June 1897 - Kuang-hsü 23, 5, 21.
From: Hu Ch'ang-t'u, Prefect, Fuchou.
To: N.A. Popoff, Consul of Russia and Denmark, Fuchou.
Communication requesting the Consul to forward two copies
of the lease of a garden to a Danish captain. The seals
of the Chinese authorities have been affixed, as the
lease has been found legal.
= 1039 Konsulatsarkiver. Foochow. Indkomne breve
m.m. 1862-93: nr. 27.

249.

Date: 22 June 1897 - Kuang-hsü 23, 5, 22.
Passport issued by the Danish Consul at Cheefoo to the Danish subject Aaberg for a trip into the interior of the Shantung province.
= 867 Konsulatsarkiver. Cheefoo 1894-1912: nr. 4.

250.

Date: (13 August 1897) - Kuang-hsü 23, 8, 16.
From: Liu, Prefect, Ching-pu prefecture.
Proclamation stating that official permission has been given to Hsieh Ping-liang (Hsieh Ju-chou), Director of the Pao-ch'eng Coal Mining Company, to start the work on the coal-mine at Pai-tiao-ling in the district of Chiang-pu in Kiangsu province.
= 2035 Konsulatsarkiver. Shanghai. Diverse korrespondance og sager 1896-98: nr. 3.

251.

Date: (15 October 1897) - (Kuang-hsü 23), 9, 20.
From: T'ang Pao-chien, Military Intendant, Fuchou.
To: N.A. Popoff, Consul of Russia and Denmark, Fuchou.
Letter stating that three money-orders from the Chinese merchant Wei Ch'in-hou have been lost and therefore have been invalidated.
Appended: A copy of the three money orders.
= 1039 Konsulatsarkiver. Foochow. Indkomne breve m.m. 1862-93: nr. 28.

252.

Date: (1898).
Copy of a letter concerning the contract between the Pao-ch'eng Coal Mining Company and a Danish subject Hakon J.H. Kirchof.
= 2035 Konsulatsarkiver. Shanghai. Korrespondancesager m.v. 1842-94: Pakke 9, nr. 39.

253.

Date: (1898).
Copy of a contract between the Pao-ch'eng Coal Mining Company and a Danish subject Hakon J.H. Kirchof concerning the management of a coal mine.
= 2035 Konsulatsarkiver. Shanghai. Korrespondancesager m.v. 1842-94: Pakke 9, nr. 35.

254.

Date: 10 January 1898 - Kuang-hsü 23, 12, 18.
Agreement between Hsieh Ju-chou, Director of the Pao-ch'eng Coal Mining Company, and Hakon J.H. Kirchof concerning the management of the coal-mine at Pai-tiao-ling in the district of Chiang-pu in Kiangsu province, for a period of 10 years.
= 2035 Konsulatsarkiver. Shanghai. Diverse Korrespondance og sager 1896-98: nr. 2.

255.

Date: 19 January 1898 - Kuang-hsü 23, 12, 27.
Contract between the Pao-ch'eng Coal Mining Company and Hearson and Company in Shanghai on sale of the materials for the work on the coal-mine in the district of Chiang-pu in Kiangsu province.
= 2035 Konsulatsarkiver. Shanghai. Diverse Korrespondance og sager 1896-98: nr. 4.

256.

Date: (16 July 1898) - Kuang-hsü 24, 5, 28.
From: Yang Wen-ting, Acting Military Intendant, Fuchou.
To: Consul of Russia and Denmark, Fuchou.
Communication notifying the Consul of the appointment of Yang Wen-ting as Manager of Trade Affairs at Fuchou. T'ang Pao-chien has been appointed Acting Provincial Judge.
= 1039 Konsulatsarkiver. Foochow. Indkomne breve m.m. 1862-93: nr. 29.

257.

Date: (1 September 1898) - Kuang-hsü 24, 7, 16.
From: Chin Hsüeh-hsien, Acting Prefect, Fuchou.
To: Consul of Russia and Denmark, Fuchou.
Communication notifying the Consul of the appointment of Chin Hsüeh-hsien as Manager of Trade Affairs at Fuchou.
= 1039 Konsulatsarkiver. Foochow. Indkomne breve m.m. 1862-93: nr. 31.

258.

Date: (18 October 1898) - Kuang-hsü 24, 9, 4.
From: Yang Wen-ting, Acting Military Intendant +
    T'ang Pao-chien, Military Intendant + Ch'en
    Ming-chih, Assistant Intendant, Fuchou.
To: Consul of Russia and Denmark, Fuchou.
Communication stating that foreign firms are warned against letting their ships and crews take part in piracy along the banks of the Min river.
= 1039 Konsulatsarkiver. Foochow. Indkomne breve m.m. 1862-93: nr. 30.

259.

Date: 2 November 1898 - Kuang-hsü 24, 9, 19.
From: Yang Wen-ting, Acting Military Intendant +
  T'ang Pao-chien, Military Intendant +
  Ch'en Ming-chih, Assistant Intendant, Fuchou.
To: Consul of Russia and Denmark, Fuchou.
Communication notifying the Consul of the appointment of the Commander-in-chief Ts'eng-Ch'i as Acting Governor-General.
= 1039 Konsulatsarkiver. Foochow. Indkomne breve m.m. 1862-93: nr. 32.

260.

Date: 16 December 1898 - Kuang-hsü 24, 11, 4.
Passport issued by the Danish Consul at Chefoo to the Danish subject Aaberg for a trip to the interior of Shantung province. Valid for three months.
Appended: A copy of the passport.
= 867 Konsulatsarkiver. Chefoo 1894-1912: nr. 2.

261.

Date: (16 December 1898) - (Kuang-hsü 24), 11, 4.
From: Li Hsi-chieh, Chefoo.
To: Consul of Russia and Denmark, Chefoo.
Letter stating that the passport issued to the Danish subject Aaberg for a trip to the interior of Shantung province has been duly stamped and is hereby returned to the Consulate.
= 867 Konsulatsarkiver. Chefoo 1894-1912: nr. 3.

262.

Date: 6 March 1899.
Agreement between China and the Great Northern Telegraph Company stating that no other party is allowed to land cables on the coast of China and the Chinese islands in competition with the existing lines.
= Store Nordiske Arkiv.

263.

Date: 15 April 1899 - Kuang-hsü 25, 3, 6.
From: Hsü Chao-feng, Transferred Prefect, Fuchou.
To: Consul of Russia and Denmark, Fuchou.
Communication notifying the Consul of the appointment of Hsü Chao-feng as Associate Manager of Trade Affairs.
= 1039 Konsulatsarkiver. Foochow. Indkomne breve m.m. 1862-93: nr. 33.

264.

Date: 18 May 1899 - Kuang-hsü 25, 4, 9.
From: Ch'en T'ung-shu, Assistant Intendant, Fuchou.
To: Consul of Russia and Denmark, Fuchou.
Communication stating that the appointment of Ch'en T'ung-shu as Manager of Foreign Affairs in Fuchou has been acknowledged by the Governor-General. The Office of Foreign Affairs will be situated at the Nan-ta road.
= 1039 Konsulatsarkiver. Foochow. Indkomne breve m.m. 1862-93: nr. 35.

265.

Date: 1 July 1899 - Kuang-hsü 25, 5, 24.
Contract between the Naval Secretaries of the Peiyang Navy, on behalf of the Governor-General of Chihli province, Yü-lu, and the Danish subject, Lieutenant C.E. Lindberg, concerning his engagement for a period of three years as a Naval Attaché to the Peiyang Naval Department.
= 2035 Konsulatsarkiver. Shanghai. Diverse Korrespondance og sager 1900-1904: nr. 1.

266.

Date: 5 August 1899 - Kuang-hsü 25, 6, 29.
From: Ch'en T'ung-shu, Assistant Intendant, Fuchou.
To: Consul of Russia and Denmark, Fuchou.
Communication stating that Imperial orders have been issued providing that an Office of Foreign Affairs be established in Fuchou. Ch'en T'ung-shu is appointed Manager of Foreign Affairs.
= 1039 Konsulatsarkiver. Foochow. Indkomne breve m.m. 1862-93: nr. 34.

267.

Date: (2 November 1899) - Kuang-hsü 25, 9, 29.
From: Ch'en T'ung-shu, Acting Salt Intendant, Fuchou.
To: N.A. Popoff, Consul of Russia and Denmark, Fuchou.
Communication notifying the Consul of the appointment of Ch'en T'ung-shu as Acting Intendant of the Salt Government and his appointment as Manager of Foreign Affairs.
= 1039 Konsulatsarkiver. Foochow. Indkomne breve m.m. 1862-93: nr. 38.

268.

Date: (8 December 1899) - Kuang-hsü 25, 11, 6.
From: Ch'en T'ung-shu, Acting Salt Intendant, Fuchou.
To: N.A. Popoff, Consul of Russia and Denmark, Fuchou.
Communication stating that Ch'en T'ung-shu has handed over the post as Intendant of the Salt Government to the recently appointed Intendant Yang Wen-ting.
= 1039 Konsulatsarkiver. Foochow. Indkomne breve m.m. 1862-93: nr. 39.

269.

Date: (17 January 1900) - Kuang-hsü 25, 12, 17.
From: Ch'en T'ung-shu, Acting Salt Intendant, Fuchou.
To: N.A. Popoff, Consul of Russia and Denmark, Fuchou.
Communication stating that according to a communication from the Consul of Great Britain, Wu Wen-chin is not a British subject but a Chinese national. Consuls are warned against surreptitious schemes for change of nationality.
= 1039 Konsulatsarkiver. Foochow. Indkomne breve m.m. 1862-93: nr. 40.

270.

Date: 20 June 1900.
Printed Proclamation notifying the Chinese people that the troops of the Allied Powers intend to use their weapons solely against the Boxers and other persons who might oppose them on their march to Peking.
= 2035 Konsulatsarkiver. Shanghai. Diverse Korrespondance og sager 1896-98: nr. 1.

271.

Date: 4 August 1900.
Agreement between China and the Great Northern Telegraph Company concerning the establishment of a telegraph-line between Shanghai and Taku.
= Store Nordiske Arkiv.

272.

Date: 26 October 1900.
Agreement between China and the Great Northern Telegraph Company concerning the re-erection of the Taku-Peking telegraph-line after the destruction caused by the Boxer rebellion.
= Store Nordiske Arkiv.

273.

Date: 26 October 1900.
Agreement between China and the Great Northern Telegraph Company concerning the telegraph-line Taku-Peking-Kiachta.
= Store Nordiske Arkiv.

274.

Date: 26 October 1900.
Agreement between China and the Great Northern Telegraph Company concerning maintenance and operation of the telegraph-line to be established between Shanghai and Taku.
= Store Nordiske Arkiv.

275.

Date: 9 February 1901.
Addenda to the agreement of 4 August 1900 between China and the Great Northern Telegraph Company concerning the establishment of a telegraph-line between Shanghai and Taku, stating that the cable between Chefoo and Taku should be provided with an additional cable.
= Store Nordiske Arkiv.

276.

Date: (12 May 1901) - (Kuang-hsü 27), 3, 24.
From: Yang Wen-ting, Provincial Judge + Ch'en T'ung-shu, Acting Grain Intendant, Fuchou.
To: Consul of Russia and Denmark, Fuchou.
Letter stating that two Imperial Edicts have been received from the Chinese Ministry of Foreign Affairs. These will be posted in the province for two years in accordance with clause 10 of the Peace Protocol of 1901.
= 1039 Konsulatsarkiver. Foochow. Indkomne breve m.m. 1862-93: nr. 37.

277.

Date: (23 September) 1901 - (Kuang-hsü 27), 8, 11.
Copy of a communication stating that the case concerning the demobilization of soldiers at Shanghai should be discussed with all governments concerned. After that the case should be negotiated between the Consul-General of Denmark, the Superintendant of Trade at the Southern Ports Sheng Hsüan-huai, and the Magistrate at Shanghai.
= 2035 Konsulatsarkiver. Shanghai. Korrespondancesager m.v. 1842-94: Pakke 9, nr. 81.

278.

Date: 27 January 1902 - (Kuang-hsü 27), 12, 20.
From: Yüan Shu-hsün, Military Intendant, Shanghai.
To: A.G.G. Leigh-Smith, Consul of Denmark, Shanghai.
Letter stating that the land leased by the Danish subject, Lindholm, has been remeasured to include the foot-path on the western side of the property and new deeds for the property have been issued by the Magistrate of the Pao-shan district. The deeds are herewith forwarded.
= 2035 Konsulatsarkiver. Shanghai. Indkomne breve 1901-1904: nr. 3.

279.

Date: (2 February 1902) - (Kuang-hsü 27), 12, 24.
From: Yüan Shu-hsün, Military Intendant, Shanghai.
To: A.G.G. Leigh-Smith, Consul of Denmark, Shanghai.
Letter stating that the previous Chinese Minister to Germany and Holland, Lü Hai-huan, will visit the Consul-General on the 6th of February 1902 at 3 p.m.
= 2035 Konsulatsarkiver. Shanghai. Indkomne breve 1901-1904: nr. 2.

280.

Date: (4 February 1902) - (Kuang-hsü 27), 12, 26.
From: Yüan Shu-hsün, Military Intendant, Shanghai.
To: A.G.G. Leigh-Smith, Consul of Denmark, Shanghai.
Letter stating that Magistrate Chang Yüan-hsing has been sent to the Ch'ung-ming district to examine the case of damage to a telegraph-cable made by the Chinese ship "Fu-shun".
= 2035 Konsulatsarkiver. Shanghai. Indkomne breve 1901-1904: nr. 1.

281.

Date: (April 1902) - Kuang-hsü 28, 3, -.
From: Ping Ke, Chefoo.
To: Consul of Russia and Denmark, Chefoo.
Petition begging the Consul to force a Danish subject to pay the sum of 50 dollars that he owes to Ping Ke for the rental of a house at Chefoo, and to make him remove his belongings from the house.
= 867 Konsulatsarkiver. Chefoo. 1894-1912: nr. 1.

282.

Date: (15 June 1902) - Kuang-hsü 28, 5, 10.
From: Yang Wen-ting, Provincial Judge + Ch'en T'ung-shu,
    Acting Grain Intendant, Fuchou.
To: Consul of Russia and Denmark, Fuchou.
Communication in reply acknowledging the receipt of a
charge of theft from the Great Northern Telegraph
Company, stating that the crew of two Chinese boats
have been caught stealing buoys and other telegraph
equipment. The case will be investigated immediately.
= 1039 Konsulatsarkiver. Foochow. Indkomne breve
m.m. 1862-93: nr. 36.

283.

Date: 22 June 1902 - Kuang-hsü 28, 5, 17.
From: Jui-Ch'ui, Military Intendant, Shanghai.
To: A.G.G. Leigh-Smith, Consul of Denmark, Shanghai.
Communication in reply stating that the Intendant has
made inquiries as to the enforced payment to the Danish
subject, Christophersen, by the Chinese subject, Huang
Ku-sun, both of whom are engaged in the tea-business at
Ningchou, of a sum of 750 taels. Difficulties have
arisen because the Consul has not stated the exact where-
abouts of Huang Ku-sun. In any case, the Magistrate of
Ningchou has been instructed to proceed with the
investigation.
= 2035 Konsulatsarkiver. Shanghai. Diverse Korrespondance
og sager 1900-1904: nr. 3.

284.

Date: 23 June 1902 - (Kuang-hsü 28), 5, 18.
From: Yüan Shu-hsün, Military Intendant, Shanghai.
To: A.G.G. Leigh-Smith, Consul of Denmark, Shanghai.
Letter stating that a letter has been received from the
Danish Consul referring to the case concerning damage
on the telegraph-cable owned by the Great Northern
Telegraph Company. The Intendant states that the proper
name of the accused is Hsi Yen-yü, captain of the boat
called "Fu-shun", not Hsi Fu-shun as stated in an
earlier communication from the Consul. Consequently,
the local authorities have been instructed to arrest Hsi
Yen-yü immediately.
= 2035 Konsulatsarkiver. Shanghai. Diverse Korrespondance
og sager 1900-1904: nr. 5.

285.

Date: 21 July 1902 - (Kuang-hsü 28), 6, 17.
From: He Fu-hai, Woosung.
To: A.G.G. Leigh-Smith, Consul of Denmark, Shanghai.
Letter stating that a joint survey will be held for the property owned by the Great Northern Telegraph Company at Woosung on the 26 of July to distinguish it from the adjacent lot owned by the Woosung Commercial Settlement.
= 2035 Konsulatsarkiver. Shanghai. Diverse Korrespondance og sager 1900-1904: nr. 2.

286.

Date: 21 October 1902 - (Kuang-hsü 28, 9, (20).
From: Chang Chen, Magistrate of the Mixed Court, Shanghai.
To: A.G.G. Leigh-Smith, Consul of Denmark, Shanghai.
Letter stating that the Magistrate Chang Chen is presently ill and therefore his duties have been transferred temporarily to the Magistrate Wei. Owing to pressing business, Wei has not yet found time to pay the Danish Consul a visit, but he intends to do so on the 23rd inst.
= 2035 Konsulatsarkiver. Shanghai. Diverse Korrespondance og sager 1900-1904: nr. 4.

287.

Date: 22 October 1902.
Revised agreement between China and the Great Northern Telegraph Company concerning the Taku-Peking-Kiachta telegraph-line, stating that an additional cable should be fastened to the poles to be used by the Great Northern Telegraph Company alone.
= Store Nordiske Arkiv.

288.

Date: (27 October 1902) - (Kuang-hsü 28), 9, 27.
Letter in reply stating that the fishermen from P'ing-t'an, who stole telegraph equipment, have not been arrested yet because two of them have emigrated and the other two are being detained in the interior of China by local officials.
= 1039 Konsulatsarkiver. Foochow. Indkomne breve m.m. 1862-93: nr. 49.

289.

Date: (24 November 1902) - (Kuang-hsü 28), 9, 25.
Letter stating that all except one of the Chinese fishermen from P'ing-t'an island who stole some telegraph equipment have escaped abroad. The fisherman who was arrested will be brought to trial. The stolen equipment has been returned to the Great Northern Telegraph Company by the relatives of the thieves.
= 1039 Konsulatsarkiver. Foochow. Indkomne breve m.m. 1862-93: nr. 50.

290.

Date: 27 December (1902) - (Kuang-hsü 28), 11, 29.
From: The Sub-Prefect, Chefoo.
To: V. de Grosse, Consul of Russia and Denmark, Chefoo.
Letter in reply stating that with reference to the case in which a messenger-runner from the Great Northern Telegraph Company, Su Ching, claims to have been assaulted by soldiers who tore off a badge with the name of the Company from his arm and molested him physically, the Chinese authorities have found out that the truth is that Su Ching was apprehended by the Chinese police while he was beating a woman in a public house late at night. When he was brought to Yamen, he received proper punishment.
= 867 Konsulatsarkiver. Chefoo. 1894-1912: nr. 5.

291.

Date: 20 March 1903 - (Kuang-hsü 29), 2, 22.
From: Yüan Shu-hsün, Military Intendant, Shanghai.
To: A.G.G. Leigh-Smith, Consul of Denmark, Shanghai.
Letter stating that the rice owned by the East Asiatic Company cannot be re-exported from the port of Shanghai because this has been prohibited by the provincial authorities on account of the rising prices of rice in the city.
= 2035 Konsulatsarkiver. Shanghai. Indkomne breve 1901-1904: nr. 4.

292.

Date: 25 March 1903 - (Kuang-hsü 29), 2, 27.
From: Lü Hai-huan + Wu T'ing-fang, Imperial Commissioners
    for Tariff Negotiations.
To: Filip Hagberg, Acting Consul of Denmark, Shanghai.
Letter stating that in accordance with Article 6 of the
Peace Protocol of 1901, the Chinese Government is presently
negotiating with the treaty powers on a raised tariff with
a five per cent import duty. As there is no Danish
Legation in Peking at present, the Chinese Ministry of
Foreign Affairs has advised the Commissioners to communicate with Filip Hagberg, the Acting Consul at Shanghai,
who is hereby requested to appoint a day for a discussion
of the matter.
= 2035 Konsulatsarkiver. Shanghai. Korrespondancesager
m.v. 1904: nr. 1A.

293.

Date: (27 March 1903) - Kuang-hsü 29, 2, 29.
From: The Office of Foreign Affairs, Fuchou.
Proclamation announcing that it is strictly prohibited to
steal telegraph equipment. The fishermen from the P'ingt'an island who stole cables and buoys last year, should
be arrested and dealt with severely.
= 1039 Konsulatsarkiver. Foochow. Indkomne breve
m.m. 1862-93: nr. 47.

294.

Date: (27 March 1903).
Copy of the Proclamation from the Office of Foreign
Affairs in Fuchou, i.e. nr. 293.
= 1039 Konsulatsarkiver. Foochow. Indkomne breve
m.m. 1862-93: nr. 48.

295.

Date: 25 August 1903 - Kuang-hsü 29, 7, 3.
From: Sheng Hsüan-huai + Lü Hai-huan + Wu T'ing-fang,
    Imperial Commissioners for Tariff Negotiations.
To: Filip Hagberg, Acting Consul of Denmark, Shanghai.
Communication stating that the Commissioners have been
informed by the Chinese Ministry of Foreign Affairs that
the Russian Ambassador at Peking has notified the
Ministry that Denmark has appointed the Acting Consul of
Denmark at Shanghai, Filip Hagberg, to negotiate the
tariff revision. The Consul is requested to consult the
representatives of the Chinese Imperial Commission,
Hippisley and Taylor, on the negotiations.
= 2035 Konsulatsarkiver. Shanghai. Korrespondancesager
m.v. 1904: nr. 18.

296.

Date: 9 January 1904 - (Kuang-hsü 29), 11, 22.
From: Yüan Shu-hsün, Military Intendant, Shanghai.
To: Peter Theodor Raaschou, Consul-General of Denmark, Shanghai.
Letter stating that the Intendant has ordered the officer from the Woosung Land Surveying Office to measure the property bought by Mr. J. Berner, an employee of the Great Northern Telegraph Company, prepare a deed for the property and thereupon send them to the office of the Intendant to be duly stamped and returned to the owner.
= 2035 Konsulatsarkiver. Shanghai. Korrespondancesager m.v. 1904: nr. 22B.

297.

Date: (22 March 1904) - Kuang-hsü 30, 2, 6.
From: Lü Hai-huan + Sheng Hsüan-huai, Imperial Commissioners of Tariff Negotiations.
To: Filip Hagberg, Consul of Denmark, Shanghai.
Communication stating that the Imperial Commissioners of Tariff Negotiations, Lü Hai-huan and Sheng Hsüan-huai, have decided to exchange the ratified Tariff-agreement between Denmark and China with Consul Filip Hagberg on the 23rd inst. at 10 o'clock in the Office of Tariff Negotiations.
= 2035 Konsulatsarkiver. Shanghai. Korrespondancesager m.v. 1904: nr. 31.

298.

Date: 10 April 1904 - (Kuang-hsü 30), 2, 25.
From: Yüan Shu-hsün, Military Intendant, Shanghai.
To: Peter Theodor Raaschou, Consul-General of Denmark, Shanghai.
Letter stating that the Magistrate Ch'en Ts'eng-p'ei has been transferred from the Land Surveying Office of Shanghai to the French Mixed Court. Magistrate Yü Tu has been appointed to the post previously filled by Ch'en.
= 2035 Konsulatsarkiver. Shanghai. Korrespondancesager m.v. 1904: nr. 10.

299.

Date: 7 May 1904 - (Kuang-hsü 30, 3), 22.
From: Lü Hai-huan + Sheng Hsüan-huai, Imperial
    Commissioners of Tariff Negotiations.
To: Peter Theodor Raaschou, Consul-General of Denmark,
    Shanghai.
Letter acknowledging the receipt of a letter from the
Danish Consul stating that a telegram has been received
from Denmark notifying the Chinese Government that the
Danish King has ratified the Tariff-agreement recently
concluded between Denmark and China.
= 2035 Konsulatsarkiver. Shanghai. Korrespondancesager
m.v. 1904: nr. 30.

300.

Date: (25 June) 1904 - (Kuang-hsü 30), 5, 12.
From: Yüan Shu-hsün, Military Intendant, Shanghai.
To: Peter Theodor Raaschou, Consul-General of Denmark,
    Shanghai.
Letter stating the exact position of the land leased by
the Great Northern Telegraph Company at Woosung. The
Land Surveying Office claims a charge for the measure-
ment of 15 dollars.
= 2035 Konsulatsarkiver. Shanghai. Korrespondancesager
m.v. 1904: nr. 22A.

301.

Date: 21 July 1904 - Kuang-hsü 30, 6, 9.
From: Kuo, Military Intendant, Chinchiang.
To: Filip Hagberg, Acting Consul of Denmark, Shanghai.
Communication stating that a letter has been received
from the Danish Consul stating that a Danish merchant,
Thomas D. Gram, intends to set up a business firm
"Hsin-t'ai-ch'ang", at Chinchiang and therefore requests
the approval of the Chinese authorities. When the case
was investigated it turned out that Mr. Gram had
reported to the authorities that he was an American
citizen and in addition had taken several other irregular
actions. Therefore the firm cannot be considered legal
and the Consul is requested to order Mr. Gram to close
down the firm immediately and wait for the decision of
the Chinese authorities.
= 2035 Konsulatsarkiver. Shanghai. Korrespondancesager
m.v. 1904: nr. 21.

302.

Date: 26 July 1904.
Agreement between China, the Great Northern Telegraph Company, the Eastern Extension Telegraph Company, the Commercial Pacific Cable Company and the Deutch-Niederlandishe Telegraphie Gesellshaft concerning the cables connected to China and concerning a joint-purse agreement. Replacing the original agreement of 11 July 1896.
= Store Nordiske Arkiv.

303.

Date: 7 September 1904 - Kuang-hsü 30, 7, 28.
From: Yüan Shu-hsün, Military Intendant, Shanghai.
To: Peter Theodor Raaschou, Consul-General of Denmark, Shanghai.
Communication stating that the Magistrate of the Pao-shan district has reported that two Chinese subjects, Tu Chin-yung and Ku Yang-ch'ing, have been arrested for immoral singing and misbehaving. They claimed that they were employed by the Great Northern Telegraph Company and the General Manager of the company, Mr. Poulsen, demanded that they should be released. The facts are that the case should be considered solely a matter of internal Chinese affairs, which the foreigners should not interfere with. The Consul is requested to instruct Mr. Poulsen to this effect.
= 2035 Konsulatsarkiver. Shanghai. Korrespondancesager m.v. 1904: nr. 101B.

304.

Date: 19 September 1904 - (Kuang-hsü 30), 8, 8.
From: Yüan Shu-hsün, Military Intendant, Shanghai.
To: Peter Theodor Raaschou, Consul-General of Denmark, Shanghai.
Letter stating that with reference to the case where Mr. Poulsen of the Great Northern Telegraph Company has complained about the arrest of two Chinese subjects to the Magistrate of the Pao-shan district, the Intendant has recently received a copy of a letter from Mr. Poulsen to the Magistrate stating that he was misinformed on the matter and is asking for an apology for his actions in this case. The Intendant therefore considers the case closed.
= 2035 Konsulatsarkiver. Shanghai. Korrespondancesager m.v. 1904: 101A.

305.

Date: 27 September 1904 - (Kuang-hsü 30), 8, 18.
From: Li Hsi-chieh, Chefoo.
To: P.H.Tiedeman, Vice-Consul of Denmark, Chefoo.
Letter in reply stating that referring to the case where a gold watch and other things were stolen from the Danish subject, Thomsen, who is employed by the Great Northern Telegraph Company, the Chinese authorities have been instructed to arrest the thief, but the investigation has not yielded any results yet.
= 867 Konsulatsarkiver. Chefoo 1894-1912: nr. 6.

306.

Date: 2 October 1904 - (Kuang-hsü 30), 8, 23.
From: Yüan Shu-hsün, Military Intendant, Shanghai.
To: Peter Theodor Raaschou, Consul-General of Denmark,
   Shanghai.
Letter stating that the deed for the property rented by a Danish merchant, L. Nellemann, has been prepared by the Land Surveying Office. The Intendant has stamped it officially and sends it enclosed in this letter. The Consul is requested to forward it to the owner.
= 2035 Konsulatsarkiver. Shanghai. Korrespondancesager m.v. 1904: nr. 32.

307.

Date: (8 October 1904) - (Kuang-hsü 30), 8, 29.
From: Teng Wen-t'o, Prefect, Shanghai.
To: Peter Theodor Raaschou, Consul-General of Denmark,
   Shanghai.
Letter stating that a report has been received stating that Yang Huan-jo has been identified as the manager of the business firm "Hsiang-yüan", which is accused by the East Asiatic Company of not having delivered the goods ordered. The "Hsiang-yüan" business firm has been closed down and the Prefect awaits orders to arrest the manager and bring him to trial.
= 2035 Konsulatsarkiver. Shanghai. Korrespondancesager m.v. 1904: nr. 1C.

308.

Date: 25 February 1905 - Kuang-hsü 31, 1, 22.
From: Yüan Shu-hsün, Military Intendant, Shanghai.
To: Peter Theodor Raaschou, Consul-General of Denmark,
   Shanghai.
Passport for Mr. Constant Alexander Krogh for a stay of one year in Mukden.
= 2035 Konsulatsarkiver. Shanghai. Korrespondancesager m.v. 1907: nr. 102.

309.

Date: (10 March 1905) - (Kuang-hsü 31), 2, 5.
From: Yüan Shu-hsün, Military Intendant, Shanghai.
To: Peter Theodor Raaschou, Consul-General of Denmark, Shanghai.
Letter stating that the appropriate authorities have been informed of the warrant of arrest issued for the Danish subject Adolf Aistrup, who is charged with embezzlement of a sum of approximately 20,000 dollars from the East Asiatic Company.
= 2035 Konsulatsarkiver. Shanghai. Korrespondancesager m.v. 1905: nr. 22.

310.

Date: 20 June 1905 - Kuang-hsü 31, 5, 17.
Passport for Mr. and Mrs. Johan Munthe-Brun for a trip to Hank'ou and Peking.
= Nationalmuseet: B 4707.

311.

Date: (19 October) 1905 - (Kuang-hsü 31), 11, 21.
From: Yüan Shu-hsün, Military Intendant, Shanghai.
To: Peter Theodor Raaschou, Consul-General of Denmark, Shanghai.
Letter stating that the Danish business firm M.L. Kristensen and Co. are allowed to import a rifle with bayonet, provided it is used only as a sample in the firm, submitted to regular inspection by the Customs, and that it cannot be sold in China on a private basis.
= 2035 Konsulatsarkiver. Shanghai. Korrespondancesager m.v. 1905: nr. 121.

312.

Date: (26 April) 1906 - (Kuang-hsü 32), 4, 3.
From: Jui-Ch'ui, Military Intendant, Shanghai.
To: Peter Theodor Raaschou, Consul-General of Denmark, Shanghai.
Letter stating that the Chinese authorities cannot issue a permit for the Danish business firm Andersen, Meyer and Co. to export living cattle to Vladivostock in order to relieve a famine there. A permit to export meat issued previously has not been used by the firm, which shows that the situation cannot be very serious.
= 2035 Konsulatsarkiver. Shanghai. Korrespondancesager m.v. 1906: nr. 48.

313.

Date: 5 June 1906 - (Kuang-hsü 32), Jun4, 13.
From: Jui-Ch'ui, Military Intendant, Shanghai.
To: Peter Theodor Raaschou, Consul-General of Denmark, Shanghai.
Letter stating that foreigners who are bringing goods into the interior of China should pay duty at the Customs, unless they have been granted a duty-free permit or transship-passes.
= 2035 Konsulatsarkiver. Shanghai. Korrespondancesager m.v. 1906: nr. 55.

314.

Date: (9 June) 1906 - (Kuang-hsü 32), Jun4, 17.
From: Jui-Ch'ui, Military Intendant, Shanghai.
To: Peter Theodor Raaschou, Consul-General of Denmark, Shanghai.
Letter stating that the two boxes with rifles and ammunition imported by the East Asiatic Company may be re-exported to Hank'ou, but the Consul should apply to the Intendant in Hank'ou for an import-permit.
= 2035 Konsulatsarkiver. Shanghai. Korrespondancesager m.v. 1906: nr. 58.

315.

Date: 29 August 1906 - (Kuang-hsü 32), 7, 10.
From: Jui-Ch'ui, Military Intendant, Shanghai.
To: Peter Theodor Raaschou, Consul-General of Denmark, Shanghai.
Letter stating that the Chinese authorities consider the Pao-shan district in the vicinity of Shanghai a part of the interior of China, where foreigners are not allowed to rent land. In addition, the land rented by the Great Northern Telegraph Company for the purpose of establishing cable-houses has been reserved for the Whampoo Water-conservancy. Therefore the Intendant cannot permit the district office to hold a survey of the land, and the Consul is requested to inform the Great Northern Telegraph Company that the renting of the land should be cancelled.
= 2035 Konsulatsarkiver. Shanghai. Korrespondancesager m.v. 1906: nr. 92.

316.

Date: 11 September 1906 - (Kuang-hsü 32), 7, 23.
From: Jui-Ch'ui, Military Intendant, Shanghai.
To: Peter Theodor Raaschou, Consul-General of Denmark, Shanghai.
Letter stating that the Danish firm Andersen, Meyer and Co. is allowed to import a small toy rifle from Germany as soon as the Customs Office has examined it and levied the appropriate duty.
= 2035 Konsulatsarkiver. Shanghai. Korrespondancesager m.v. 1906: nr. 104B.

317.

Date: 19 September 1906 - (Kuang-hsü 32), 8, 2.
From: Jui-Ch'ui, Military Intendant, Shanghai.
To: Peter Theodor Raaschou, Consul-General of Denmark, Shanghai.
Letter stating that Baron Haxthausen has requested permission to import 15 pistols and four boxes with ammunition for the purpose of showing them to the military authorities of China. The request cannot be granted because pistols cannot be imported into China unless this has been approved by the Chinese authorities.
= 2035 Konsulatsarkiver. Shanghai. Korrespondancesager m.v. 1906: nr. 106.

318.

Date: 11 October 1906 - Kuang-hsü 32, 8, 24.
Passport for the Danish missionary, N. Kristiansen, for a journey to the Liaoning province.
= 2035 Konsulatsarkiver. Shanghai. Korrespondancesager m.v. 1911: nr. 10B.

319.

Date: (14 October 1906) - Kuang-hsü 32, 8, 27.
From: Jui-Ch'ui, Military Intendant, Shanghai.
To: Peter Theodor Raaschou, Consul-General of Denmark, Shanghai.
Communication stating that orders have been received from the Governor of Anhui province requesting that the Consuls will impress on the commanders of foreign ships that they should take care that the members of the crew do not go hunting in the areas along the banks of the Yangtse River. An English officer has recently wounded a Chinese subject during such a hunt.
= 2035 Konsulatsarkiver. Shanghai. Korrespondancesager m.v. 1906: nr. 122.

320.

Date: December 1906.
From: Lu Li-hsien, Shanghai.
To: Peter Theodor Raaschou, Consul-General of Denmark, Shanghai.
Petition asking the Consul to make sure that Lu Li-hsien be repaid a debt of 1740 dollars that the late Mr. A. Bidoulac, a Danish lawyer at Shanghai, owes to him from the time Lu Li-hsien was a comprador in Mr. Bidoulac's firm.
= 2035 Konsulatsarkiver. Shanghai. Korrespondancesager m.v. 1906: nr. 28.

321.

Date: (1907).
From: Jui-Ch'ui, Military Intendant, Shanghai.
To: Consul of Denmark, Shanghai.
Letter inviting the Consul of Denmark to the Magistrate's Office to receive the congratulations of the Shanghai officials on the birthday of the Danish King.
= 2035 Konsulatsarkiver. Shanghai. Korrespondancesager m.v. 1842-94: Pakke 9, nr. 51.

322.

Date: (1907).
From: Jui-Ch'ui, Military Intendant, Shanghai.
To: Peter Theodor Raaschou, Consul-General of Denmark, Shanghai.
Letter stating that the boxes with guns and ammunition can pass the Customs if the Great Northern Telegraph Company will warrant that they will only be used by the employees of the Company for their own protection.
= 2035 Konsulatsarkiver. Shanghai. Korrespondancesager m.v. 1842-94: Pakke 9, nr. 84.

323.

Date: (1907).
From: Jui Ch'ui, Military Intendant, Shanghai.
To: Peter Theodor Raaschou, Consul-General of Denmark, Shanghai.
Letter in reply stating that more information is required concerning the destination of the boxes with airguns before they can pass the Customs.
= 2035 Konsulatsarkiver. Shanghai. Korrespondancesager m.v. 1842-94: Pakke 9, nr. 85.

324.

Date: 11 January 1907 - (Kuang-hsü 32), 11, 27.
From: Jui-Ch'ui, Military Intendant, Shanghai.
To: Peter Theodor Raaschou, Consul-General of Denmark,
    Shanghai.
Letter stating that instructions have been received
from the Superintendant of Trade at the Southern Ports
Tuan-Fang inviting the Danish Prince Valdemar, whom he
met during his visit to Denmark in the spring 1905, to
visit Tuan-Fang in Nanking during the journey of the
Prince to China and Japan.
= 2035 Konsulatsarkiver. Shanghai. Korrespondancesager
m.v. 1906: nr. 128.

325.

Date: 20 January 1907 - (Kuang-hsü 32), 12, 7.
From: Jui-Ch'ui, Military Intendant, Shanghai.
To: Peter Theodor Raaschou, Consul-General of Denmark,
    Shanghai.
Letter stating that permission to import two pieces of
spelter requested by the Danish firm Andersen, Meyer and
Co. cannot be granted because an approval from the
Chinese military authorities is required before arms can
be imported.
= 2035 Konsulatsarkiver. Shanghai. Korrespondancesager
m.v. 1907: nr. 1.

326.

Date: 24 February 1907 - Kuang-hsü 33, 1, 12.
From: Jui-Ch'ui, Military Intendant, Shanghai.
To: Peter Theodor Raaschou, Consul-General of Denmark,
    Shanghai.
Communication notifying the Consul that Jui-Ch'ui is to
travel to Nanking on official business.
= 2035 Konsulatsarkiver. Shanghai. Korrespondancesager
m.v. 1907: nr. 75.

327.

Date: (9 March) 1907 - (Kuang-hsü 33), 1, 25.
From: Jui-Ch'ui, Military Intendant, Shanghai.
To: Peter Theodor Raaschou, Consul-General of Denmark,
    Shanghai.
Letter stating that in accordance with instructions from
the Ministry of Foreign Affairs, the Chinese authorities
request the Consul to prepare a list of the names and the
dates of arrival to the posts for the Consul, the Vice-
Consul and other personnel at the Consulate.
= 2035 Konsulatsarkiver. Shanghai. Korrespondancesager
m.v. 1907: nr. 52A.

328.

Date: 27 April 1907 - (Kuang-hsü 33), 3, 15.
From: Jui-Ch'ui, Military Intendant, Shanghai.
To: Peter Theodor Raaschou, Consul-General of Denmark, Shanghai.
Letter requesting the Consul to forward the particulars concerning the Consulate, such as the names, dates of appointment, etc. for the personnel at the Consulate. The information is needed for a report to the Ministry of Foreign Affairs.
= 2035 Konsulatsarkiver. Shanghai. Korrespondancesager m.v. 1907: nr. 52B.

329.

Date: 29 April 1907 - Kuang-hsü 33, 3, 17.
From: Jui-Ch'ui, Military Intendant, Shanghai.
To: Peter Theodor Raaschou, Consul-General of Denmark, Shanghai.
Communication notifying the Consul that Jui-Ch'ui is to travel to Nanking on official business.
= 2035 Konsulatsarkiver. Shanghai. Korrespondancesager m.v. 1907: nr. 63.

330.

Date: 20 May 1907 - Kuang-hsü 33, 4, 9.
From: Jui-Ch'ui, Military Intendant, Shanghai.
To: Peter Theodor Raaschou, Consul-General of Denmark, Shanghai.
Communication notifying the Consul that Jui-Ch'ui is to travel to Suchou and Nanking on official business.
= 2035 Konsulatsarkiver. Shanghai. Korrespondancesager m.v. 1907: nr. 80A.

331.

Date: 24 May 1907 - Kuang-hsü 33, 4, 13.
From: Jui-Ch'ui, Military Intendant, Shanghai.
To: Peter Theodor Raaschou, Consul-General of Denmark, Shanghai.
Communication notifying the Consul that Jui-Ch'ui has returned from a trip to Suchou and Nanking on official business.
= 2035 Konsulatsarkiver. Shanghai. Korrespondancesager m.v. 1907: nr. 80B.

332.

Date: (28 June 1907) - (Kuang-hsü 33), 5, 18.
From: Jui-Ch'ui, Military Intendant, Shanghai.
To: Peter Theodor Raaschou, Consul-General of Denmark, Shanghai.
Letter stating that a petition has been received from 20 Chinese subjects living in the vicinity of Shanghai who have complained that foreigners who are hunting dogs in the area often accidentally shoot at Chinese people. Recently a foreigner shot two women from Fa-hua village. The Consul is requested to instruct foreigners not to go hunting in the area, otherwise trouble with the local population can be expected.
= 2035 Konsulatsarkiver. Shanghai. Korrespondancesager m.v. 1907: nr. 73.

333.

Date: (4 July 1907) - Kuang-hsü 33, 5, 24.
From: Lü Hai-huan + Sheng Hsüan-huai, Imperial Commissioners of Tariff Negotiations.
To: Peter Theodor Raaschou, Consul-General of Denmark, Shanghai.
Communication stating that Lu Hai-huan has been appointed to a post at the Chinese Ministry of Foreign Affairs. Sheng Hsüan-huai remains at the post as Imperial Commissioner of Tariff Negotiations.
= 2035 Konsulatsarkiver. Shanghai. Korrespondancesager m.v. 1907: nr. 93.

334.

Date: (2 August) 1907 - (Kuang-hsü 33), 6, 24.
From: Kuan Chiung, Intendant, Ningpo.
To: Peter Theodor Raaschou, Consul-General of Denmark, Shanghai.
Letter stating that with reference to the case of the Danish firm E.S. Petersen and Co. which has accused a Chinese merchant of fraud, the Intendant Kuan Chiung has already prepared a Chinese notice concerning the matter, but since the Consulate has no interpreters at the moment, a notice in a Western language has been prepared and signed and is forwarded enclosed.
= 2035 Konsulatsarkiver. Shanghai. Korrespondancesager m.v. 1904: nr. 104.

335.

Date: (13 August 1907) - Kuang-hsü 33, 7, 5.
From: Jui-Ch'ui, Military Intendant, Shanghai.
To: Peter Theodor Raaschou, Consul-General of Denmark, Shanghai.
Communication stating that Jui-Ch'ui is to travel to Suchou on official business.
= 2035 Konsulatsarkiver. Shanghai. Korrespondancesager m.v. 1842-94: Pakke 9, nr. 78.

336.

Date: (14 August 1907) - (Kuang-hsü 33), 7, 6.
From: Yü Chao-fan, Intendant, Ningpo.
To: Peter Theodor Raaschou, Consul-General of Denmark, Shanghai.
Letter stating that with reference to the dispute between the Danish firm E.S. Petersen and Co. and its agent at Ningpo, Li Shu-t'ang, a petition has been received from the Chinese merchant stating that he was withheld the payment of tls. 407.51 because the Danish firm has not forwarded the monthly payment of 300 dollars for the last three months as it should according to an agreement between E.S. Petersen and Co. and Li Shu-t'ang. The Intendant proposes that both parties pay their debts so that the case can be settled peacefully.
= 2035 Konsulatsarkiver. Shanghai. Korrespondancesager m.v. 1907: nr. 104B.

337.

Date: (17 August 1907) - Kuang-hsü 33, 7, 9.
From: Jui-Ch'ui, Military Intendant, Shanghai.
To: Peter Theodor Raaschou, Consul-General of Denmark, Shanghai.
Communication stating that Jui-Ch'ui has returned to his office after a trip to Nanking on official business.
= 2035 Konsulatsarkiver. Shanghai. Korrespondancesager m.v. 1842-94: Pakke 9, nr. 80.

338.

Date: (19 August) 1907 - (Kuang-hsü 33), 7, 11.
From: Jui-Ch'ui, Military Intendant, Shanghai.
To: Peter Theodor Raaschou, Consul-General of Denmark, Shanghai.
Letter stating that if the Customs should be able to grant a duty-free permit for the two boxes with airguns imported by the Danish firm Andersen, Meyer and Co., the firm should present an import-permit from the place where the boxes are to be re-exported.
= 2035 Konsulatsarkiver. Shanghai. Korrespondancesager m.v. 1907: nr. 103A.

339.

Date: (29 August 1907) - Kuang-hsü 33, 7, 21.
From: Jui-Ch'ui, Military Intendant, Shanghai.
To: Peter Theodor Raaschou, Consul-General of Denmark,
    Shanghai.
Communication stating that Jui-Ch'ui is to travel to
T'ung-chou to examine the construction of a Customs-
house.
= 2035 Konsulatsarkiver. Shanghai. Korrespondancesager
m.v. 1842-94: Pakke 9, nr. 79.

340.

Date: (4 September) 1907 - (Kuang-hsü 33), 7, 27.
From: Jui-Ch'ui, Military Intendant, Shanghai.
To: Peter Theodor Raaschou, Consul-General of Denmark,
    Shanghai.
Letter stating that a communication has been received
from the Consul stating that the two boxes with airguns
are to be re-exported to Hankou and requesting that a
duty-free permit be issued by the Customs. The Intendant
is obliged to stress again that he has to get an import-
permit from the Intendant of Hank'ou before he can issue a
duty-free permit.
= 2035 Konsulatsarkiver. Shanghai. Korrespondancesager
m.v. 1907: nr. 103B.

341.

Date: (10 September 1907) - Kuang-hsü 33, 8, 3.
From: Jui-Ch'ui, Military Intendant, Shanghai.
To: Peter Theodor Raaschou, Consul-General of Denmark,
    Shanghai.
Communication stating that Jui-Ch'ui has returned from a
trip to T'ung-chou on official business.
= 2035 Konsulatsarkiver. Shanghai. Korrespondancesager
m.v. 1908: nr. 233A.

342.

Date:(11 September 1907) - (Kuang-hsü 33), 8, 4.
From: Yü Chao-fan, Intendant, Ningpo.
To: Peter Theodor Raaschou, Consul-General of Denmark,
    Shanghai.
Letter acknowledging that the Consul has delivered the
cheque for 47.26 tls. to the foreign business firm
"He-p'ing". With reference to the importation of wheat
flour, the Intendant has been notified by the Ministry
of Foreign Affairs that according to the tariffs a duty
of 0.10 tael for every 100 catty of wheat flour should
be paid to the Customs.
= 2035 Konsulatsarkiver. Shanghai. Korrespondancesager
m.v. 1907: nr. 104A.

343.

Date: (13 September 1907) - (Kuang-hsü 33), 9, 14.
From: Pao Yi, Magistrate at the Mixed Court, Shanghai.
To: Peter Theodor Raaschou, Consul-General of Denmark, Shanghai.
Letter stating that on account of the appointment of Pao-Yi to the post as Magistrate at the Mixed Court, he intends to visit the Consulate on the 15th inst.
= 2035 Konsulatsarkiver. Shanghai. Korrespondancesager m.v. 1908: L. nr. 3.

344.

Date: (26 September) 1907 - (Kuang-hsü 33), 8, 19.
From: Kuan Chiung, Magistrate of the Mixed Court, Shanghai.
To: Peter Theodor Raaschou, Consul-General of Denmark, Shanghai.
Letter stating that the Mixed Court will settle the case of the Danish business firm E.S. Petersen and Co. which has accused Hsieh Chin-jung for the theft of a cash-book on the 26th inst.
= 2035 Konsulatsarkiver. Shanghai. Korrespondancesager m.v. 1907: nr. 35.

345.

Date: (2 October 1907) - Kuang-hsü 33, 8, 25.
From: Hsin Ch'in, Commander-in-chief.
To: Peter Theodor Raaschou, Consul-General of Denmark, Shanghai.
Communication notifying the appointment of Hsin Ch'in as Acting Governor of Chekiang.
= 2035 Konsulatsarkiver. Shanghai. Korrespondancesager m.v. 1842-94: Pakke 9, nr. 32.

346.

Date: (9 October 1907) - Kuang-hsü 33, 9, 3.
From: Jui-Ch'ui, Military Intendant, Shanghai.
To: Peter Theodor Raaschou, Consul-General of Denmark, Shanghai.
Communication stating that Jui-Ch'ui is to travel to Suchou on official business.
= 2035 Konsulatsarkiver. Shanghai. Korrespondancesager m.v. 1908: nr. 233B.

347.

Date: (14 October 1907) - Kuang-hsü 33, 9, 8.
From: Jui-Ch'ui, Military Intendant, Shanghai.
To: Peter Theodor Raaschou, Consul-General of Denmark, Shanghai.
Communication stating that Jui-Ch'ui has returned from a trip to Suchou on official business.
= 2035 Konsulatsarkiver. Shanghai. Korrespondancesager m.v. 1908: nr. 233D.

348.

Date: (16 October 1907) - (Kuang-hsü 33), 9, 10.
From: Jui-Ch'ui, Military Intendant, Shanghai.
To: Peter Theodor Raaschou, Consul-General of Denmark, Shanghai.
Letter stating that orders have been received from the Governor-General Tuan-Fang stating that the Chinese merchants Sun Fu-hsiang and others have started the Water-works Company at Chinchiang without the proper registration at the Magistrate's Office. The Company is therefore illegal and the contract between the Company and a foreign business firm concerning supply of machinery should be cancelled.
= 2035 Konsulatsarkiver. Shanghai. Korrespondancesager m.v. 1907: nr. 135.

349.

Date: (20 October 1907) - (Kuang-hsü 33), 9, 14.
From: Jui-Ch'ui, Military Intendant, Shanghai.
To: Peter Theodor Raaschou, Consul-General of Denmark, Shanghai.
Letter stating that if the Danish firm Andersen, Meyer and Co. wishes to import two rifles and 500 cartridges according to rule no. 2 of the new Regulations for Importation of Arms and Ammunition, it should supply the necessary information in regard to which Chinese official is to purchase them.
= 2035 Konsulatsarkiver. Shanghai. Korrespondancesager m.v. 1907: nr. 124A.

350.

Date: (26 October 1907) - Kuang-hsü 33, 9, 20.
From: Wang Hsieh, Acting Military Intendant, Shanghai.
To: Peter Theodor Raaschou, Consul-General of Denmark, Shanghai.
Communication stating that Wang Hsieh takes charge temporarily of the post as Military Intendant and Inspector of Customs in Shanghai because Jui-Ch'ui has been posted elsewhere.
= 2035 Konsulatsarkiver. Shanghai. Korrespondancesager m.v. 1908. nr. 233G.

351.

Date: (4 November 1907) - (Kuang-hsü 33), 9, 29.
From: Wang Hsieh, Intendant, Shanghai.
To: Peter Theodor Raaschou, Consul-General of Denmark, Shanghai.
Letter stating that the Danish firm Andersen, Meyer and Co. is granted permission to import two rifles and cartridges as a sample if the Consul guarantees that the rifles are kept in custody at the firm and are not used for other purposes. According to the new rules, however, rifles are not allowed to be imported even as samples unless official Chinese authorities issue a special permit.
= 2035 Konsulatsarkiver. Shanghai. Korrespondancesager m.v. 1907: nr. 124B.

352.

Date: (7 November 1907) - Kuang-hsü 33, 10, 2.
From: Wang Hsieh, Acting Military Intendant, Shanghai.
To: Peter Theodor Raaschou, Consul-General of Denmark, Shanghai.
Communication stating that Wang Hsieh is to travel to Suchou and Nanking on official business.
= 2035 Konsulatsarkiver. Shanghai. Korrespondancesager m.v. 1908: nr. 233E.

353.

Date: (10 November 1907) - Kuang-hsü 33, 10, 5.
From: Wang Hsieh, Deputy Military Intendant, Shanghai.
To: Peter Theodor Raaschou, Consul-General of Denmark, Shanghai.
Communication stating that Wang Hsieh has returned from a trip to Suchou on official business.
= Konsulatsarkiver. Shanghai. Korrespondancesager m.v. 1842-94: Pakke 9, nr. 33.

354.

Date: (15 November 1907) - (Kuang-hsü 33), 10, 10.
From: Wang Hsieh, Acting Military Intendant, Shanghai.
To: Wilhelm Meyer, Vice-Consul of Denmark, Shanghai.
Two letters stating that Wang Hsieh will receive visits and congratulations on the birthday of the Empress Dowager.
= 2035 Konsulatsarkiver. Shanghai. Korrespondancesager m.v. 1908: nr. 233H.

355.

Date: (19 November 1907) - (Kuang-hsü 33), 10, 14.
From: Wang Hsieh, Military Intendant, Shanghai.
To: Peter Theodor Raaschou, Consul-General of Denmark, Shanghai.
Letter stating that a letter has been received from the Consul stating that the rifles and cartridges imported by the Danish firm Andersen, Meyer and Co. had reached the port before the new rules were implemented and that they are to be used as samples only and are not for sale. The Intendant has accordingly issued orders to the Customs to prepare an import-permit.
= 2035 Konsulatsarkiver. Shanghai. Korrespondancesager m.v. 1907: nr. 124C.

356.

Date: (22 November 1907) - (Kuang-hsü 33), 10, 17.
From: Wang Hsieh, Acting Military Intendant, Shanghai.
To: Peter Theodor Raaschou, Consul-General of Denmark, Shanghai.
Letter stating that an American missionary who has settled on some land at Ma-lu has not paid taxes. The Intendant has brought the case up in the court.
= 2035 Konsulatsarkiver. Shanghai. Korrespondancesager m.v. 1908: nr. 233F.

357.

Date: (24 November 1907) - Kuang-hsü 33, 10, 19.
From: Liang Ju-hao, Military Intendant, Shanghai.
To: Peter Theodor Raaschou, Consul-General of Denmark, Shanghai.
Communication notifying the Consul of the appointment of Liang Ju-hao, who assumes the post previously managed by Wang Hsieh.
= 2035 Konsulatsarkiver. Shanghai. Korrespondancesager m.v. 1842-94: Pakke 9, nr. 31.

358.

Date: (25 November 1907) - (Kuang-hsü 33), 10, 20.
From: Liang Ju-hao, Military Intendant, Shanghai.
To: Peter Theodor Raaschou, Consul-General of Denmark, Shanghai.
Letter stating that the Consul-General has requested that passes for travel in South Manchuria should be issued for five Danish missionaries. The Intendant states that the common procedure for such passes is that the passes are issued by the Consulate and then given the official stamp by the Intendant.
= 2035 Konsulatsarkiver. Shanghai. Korrespondancesager m.v. 1907: nr. 142.

359.

Date: (25 November 1907) - (Kuang-hsü 33), 10, 20.
From: Liang Ju-hao, Military Intendant, Shanghai.
To: Peter Theodor Raaschou, Consul-General of Denmark, Shanghai.
Letter stating that the toy guns imported by the Danish firm Andersen, Meyer and Co. can be re-exported to Tientsin if the Consul can obtain an import-permit from the Intendant of Tientsin.
= 2035 Konsulatsarkiver. Shanghai. Korrespondancesager m.v. 1907: nr. 146B.

360.

Date: (25 November 1907) - (Kuang-hsü 33), 10, 20.
From: Liang Ju-hao, Military Intendant, Shanghai.
To: Peter Theodor Raaschou, Consul-General of Denmark, Shanghai.
Letter stating that the Consul has requested that the import-permit issued for two sample guns and 500 cartridges imported by the Danish firm Andersen, Meyer and Co. should be changed to a permit for 750 cartridges. The Intendant proposes that the surplus of the cartridges should be confiscated in order to avoid misuse of the new Regulations for Importation of Arms and Ammunition.
= 2035 Konsulatsarkiver. Shanghai. Korrespondancesager m.v. 1907: nr. 146A.

361.

Date: (26 November 1907) - (Kuang-hsü 33), 10, 21.
From: Liang Ju-hao, Military Intendant, Shanghai.
To: Peter Theodor Raaschou, Consul-General of Denmark, Shanghai.
Letter stating that Liang Ju-hao has taken over the post as Military Intendant and Inspector of Customs at Shanghai. He intends to visit the Consulate on the 28th inst.
= 2035 Konsulatsarkiver. Shanghai. Korrespondancesager m.v. 1908: nr. 233C.

362.

Date: (4 December 1907) - (Kuang-hsü 33), 10, 29.
From: Pao Yi, Magistrate of the Mixed Court, Shanghai.
To: Peter Theodor Raaschou, Consul-General of Denmark, Shanghai.
Letter stating that the Magistrate Pao Yi intends to visit the Consulate on the 6th to discuss the case E.S. Petersen and Co. vs. Hsieh Chin-jung.
= 2035 Konsulatsarkiver. Shanghai. Korrespondancesager m.v. 1907: nr. 132A.

363.

Date: (23 December 1907) - (Kuang-hsü 33), 11, 19.
From: Liang Ju-hao, Military Intendant, Shanghai.
To: Peter Theodor Raaschou, Consul-General of Denmark, Shanghai.
Letter stating that the official business of the Land Surveying Office of Shanghai will be supervised by Wu Yüan, a representative of the Intendant's office.
= 2035 Konsulatsarkiver. Shanghai. Korrespondancesager m.v. 1908: nr. 233I.

364.

Date: (31 December 1907).
New Year Greetings and visiting cards from the Chinese officials in Shanghai.
= 2035 Konsulatsarkiver. Shanghai. Korrespondancesager m.v. 1907: New Year Greetings.

365.

Date: (1908).
Letter acknowledging the receipt of the condolences presented by the Danish Consul on the occasion of the death of the Empress Dowager Tz'u-hsi and the Kuang-hsü Emperor.
= 2035 Konsulatsarkiver. Shanghai. Korrespondancesager m.v. 1908: L. nr. 58.

366.

Date: (1908).
From: Ch'en Ch'i-t'ai, Governor, Suchou.
To: Peter Theodor Raaschou, Consul-General of Denmark, Shanghai.
Letter acknowledging the receipt of the condolences presented by the Danish Consul on the occasion of the death of the Empress Dowager Tz'u-hsi and the Kuang-hsü Emperor.
= 2035 Konsulatsarkiver. Shanghai. Korrespondancesager m.v. 1908: L nr. 57.

367.

Date: (1908).
Letter stating that the Governor-General Tuan-Fang wishes to express his thanks for the letter of condolences sent by the Danish Consul on the occasion of the death of the wife of the uncle of Tuan-Fang.
= 2035 Konsulatsarkiver. Shanghai. Korrespondancesager m.v. 1908: L. nr. 42.

368.

Date: 1908.
From: Hu T'iao-yüan, Magistrate of the Pao-shan district.
To: Peter Theodor Raaschou, Consul-General of Denmark,
    Shanghai.
Letter inquiring whether any foreigners have bought a
strip of land in the Pao-shan district. In case foreigners
have bought land, they should pay the land tax to the
Magistrate's Office immediately.
= 2035 Konsulatsarkiver. Shanghai. Korrespondancesager
m.v. 1908: nr. 82A.

369.

Date: 1908.
From: Hu T'iao-yüan, Magistrate of the Pao-shan district.
To: Peter Theodor Raaschou, Consul-General of Denmark,
    Shanghai.
Letter stating that if any foreigners have bought land in
the Pao-shan district, the Consul is requested to forward
a list of their names etc. so that the land tax can be
collected.
= 2035 Konsulatsarkiver. Shanghai. Korrespondancesager
m.v. 1908: nr. 82B.

370.

Date: (26 January 1908) - (Kuang-hsü 33), 12, 23.
From: Liang Ju-hao, Military Intendant, Shanghai.
To: Peter Theodor Raaschou, Consul-General of Denmark,
    Shanghai.
Letter stating that with reference to the Chinese
soldiers who stole a cargo of 1000 bags of flour from a
junk in the harbour of Cha-p'u, the crime has been
committed in an area which is under the jurisdiction of
the Governor of Chekiang, whom the Intendant has informed
of the matter.
= 2035 Konsulatsarkiver. Shanghai. Korrespondancesager
m.v. 1908: nr. 8A.

371.

Date: (28 January 1908) - (Kuang-hsü 33), 12, 25.
From: Pao Yi, Magistrate of the Mixed Court, Shanghai.
To: Peter Theodor Raaschou, Consul-General of Denmark,
    Shanghai.
Letter stating that the Magistrate Pao Yi intends to
visit the Consulate on the 29th to discuss the case
between the Danish firm E.S. Petersen and Co. vs. Hsieh
Chin-jung.
= 2035 Konsulatsarkiver. Shanghai. Korrespondancesager
m.v. 1907: nr. 132B.

372.

Date: (1 February 1908) - (Kuang-hsü 33), 12, 29.
From: Liang Ju-hao, Military Intendant, Shanghai.
To: Peter Theodor Raaschou, Consul-General of Denmark,
    Shanghai.
Letter stating that with reference to the incident where a cargo of 1000 bags of flour which was owned by the Danish firm Hillebrandt and Co. was stolen by Chinese soldiers from a junk in the harbour of Cha-p'u, the Intendant has informed the Intendant of Hangchou of the matter and requested that he make sure that the flour is returned to the Company and that the soldiers in question are punished.
= 2035 Konsulatsarkiver. Shanghai. Korrespondancesager m.v. 1908: nr. 8B.

373.

Date: (10 February 1908) - Kuang-hsü 34, 1, 9.
From: Liang Ju-hao, Military Intendant, Shanghai.
To: Peter Theodor Raaschou, Consul-General of Denmark,
    Shanghai.
Communication stating that Liang Ju-hao is to travel to Nanking on official business.
= 2035 Konsulatsarkiver. Shanghai. Korrespondancesager m.v. 1908: L. nr. 9.

374.

Date: (18 February 1908) - Kuang-hsü 34, 1, 17.
From: Liang Ju-hao, Military Intendant, Shanghai.
To: Peter Theodor Raaschou, Consul-General of Denmark,
    Shanghai.
Communication stating that Liang Ju-hao has returned from a trip to Nanking on official business.
= 2035 Konsulatsarkiver. Shanghai. Korrespondancesager m.v. 1908: L. nr. 18.

375.

Date: (March 1908).
From: Jui-Ch'ui, Military Intendant, Shanghai.
To: Peter Theodor Raaschou, Consul-General of Denmark,
    Shanghai.
Letter stating that Jui-Ch'ui asks the Consul to forgive him for not visiting the Consulate when he came back from Suchou last month.
= 2035 Konsulatsarkiver. Shanghai. Korrespondancesager m.v. 1908: L. nr. 19.

376.

Date: (6 April 1908) - Kuang-hsü 34, 3, 6.
From: Jui-Ch'ui, Military Intendant, Shanghai.
To: Peter Theodor Raaschou, Consul-General of Denmark,
    Shanghai.
Communication notifying the Consul of the appointment of
Ts'ai Nai-huang to the post of Military Intendant and
Inspector of Customs at Shanghai.
= 2035 Konsulatsarkiver. Shanghai. Korrespondancesager
m.v. 1908: L. nr. 16.

377.

Date: (6 April 1908) - (Kuang-hsü 34), 3, 6.
From: Ts'ai Nai-huang, Military Intendant, Shanghai.
To: Peter Theodor Raaschou, Consul-General of Denmark,
    Shanghai.
Letter stating that on account of the appointment of
Ts'ai Nai-huang to the post of Military Intendant at Shanghai
he intends to visit the Consulate on the 8th.
= 2035 Konsulatsarkiver. Shanghai. Korrespondancesager
m.v. 1908: L. nr. 17.

378.

Date: (22 April 1908) - Kuang-hsü 34, 3, 22.
From: Ts'ai Nai-huang, Military Intendant, Shanghai.
To: Peter Theodor Raaschou, Consul-General of Denmark,
    Shanghai.
List of the winning numbers in the Anwei Railway Lottery.
= 2035 Konsulatsarkiver. Shanghai. Korrespondancesager
m.v. 1908: nr. 204.

379.

Date: (26 April 1908) - Kuang-hsü 34, 3, 26.
From: Ts'ai Nai-huang, Military Intendant, Shanghai.
To: Peter Theodor Raaschou, Consul-General of Denmark,
    Shanghai.
Communication stating that Ts'ai Nai-huang is to travel to
Nanking on official business.
= 2035 Konsulatsarkiver. Shanghai. Korrespondancesager
m.v. 1908: L. nr. 24.

380.

Date: (29 April 1908) - Kuang-hsü 34, 3, 29.
From: Ts'ai Nai-huang, Military Intendant, Shanghai.
To: Peter Theodor Raaschou, Consul-General of Denmark, Shanghai.
Communication stating that Ts'ai Nai-huang has returned from a trip to Nanking on official business.
= 2035 Konsulatsarkiver. Shanghai. Korrespondancesager m.v. 1908: L. nr. 23.

381.

Date: (30 April 1908) - (Kuang-hsü 34), 4, 1.
From: Ts'ai Nai-huang, Military Intendant, Shanghai.
To: Peter Theodor Raaschou, Consul-General of Denmark, Shanghai.
Letter stating that the deputy of the Shanghai Land Surveying Office, Wu Yüan-chi, has been transferred to a post in Chihli province. Huang Tsan-ch'ao has been appointed to the vacant post.
= 2035 Konsulatsarkiver. Shanghai. Korrespondancesager m.v. 1908: L. nr. 20.

382.

Date: (4 May 1908) - (Kuang-hsü 34), 4, 5.
From: The Sub-Prefect, Chefoo.
To: C.P. Kristy, Vice-Consul of Denmark, Chefoo.
Letter stating that referring to the case of the servant T'ang Feng-kang, who is accused of having stolen some money etc. from the Danish subject, Schwensen, an employee of the Great Northern Telegraph Company, T'ang Feng-kang has now been questioned several times but still claims that he is innocent.
= 867 Konsulatsarkiver. Chefoo. 1894-1912: nr. 8.

383.

Date: (20 May 1908) - Kuang-hsü 34, 4, 21.
From: Ts'ai Nai-huang, Military Intendant, Shanghai.
To: Peter Theodor Raaschou, Consul-General of Denmark, Shanghai.
Communication stating that Ts'ai Nai-huang is to travel to Nanking on official business.
= 2035 Konsulatsarkiver. Shanghai. Korrespondancesager m.v. 1908: L. nr. 21.

384.

Date: (23 May 1908) - Kuang-hsü 34, 4, 24.
From: Ts'ai Nai-huang, Military Intendant, Shanghai.
To: Peter Theodor Raaschou, Consul-General of Denmark, Shanghai.
Communication stating that Ts'ai Nai-huang has returned from a trip to Nanking on official business.
= 2035 Konsulatsarkiver. Shanghai. Korrespondancesager m.v. 1908: L. nr. 22.

385.

Date: (24 May 1908) - (Kuang-hsü 34), 4, 25.
From: Ts'ai Nai-huang, Military Intendant, Shanghai.
To: Peter Theodor Raaschou, Consul-General of Denmark, Shanghai.
Letter stating that the Consul is requested to send a Chinese passport for the Danish missionary, Miss Augusta Wied, so that the Intendant can stamp it officially.
= 2035 Konsulatsarkiver. Shanghai. Korrespondancesager m.v. 1908: nr. 25B.

386.

Date: (26 May 1908) - (Kuang-hsü 34), 4, 27.
From: Pao Yi, Magistrate of the Mixed Court, Shanghai.
To: Peter Theodor Raaschou, Consul-General of Denmark, Shanghai.
Letter stating that the Magistrate has issued a summons for the owners of the two Chinese firms "Pao-hung" and "Heng-Sheng", which have been sued by the Danish firm Hillebrandt and Co. for lack of delivery of goods.
= 2035 Konsulatsarkiver. Shanghai. Korrespondancesager m.v. 1908: nr. 72D.

387.

Date: (27 May 1908) - Kuang-hsü 34, 4, 28.
Petition from the Danish firm Hillebrandt and Co. requesting for the second time that the owner of the Chinese firm "Pao-hung", T'ang He-lou, be summoned to court.
= 2035 Konsulatsarkiver. Shanghai. Korrespondancesager m.v. 1908: nr. 72F.

388.

Date: (28 May 1908) - (Kuang-hsü 34), 4, 29.
From: Pao Yi, Magistrate of the Mixed Court, Shanghai.
To: Peter Theodor Raaschou, Consul-General of Denmark,
    Shanghai.
Letter stating that the defendant in the case of Hillebrandt and Co. vs. Huang Mao-chi has been summoned to the Mixed Court, but the representative of the Magistrate has been told by the relatives of the defendant that he has gone to Nanking.
= 2035 Konsulatsarkiver. Shanghai. Korrespondancesager m.v. 1908: nr. 72A.

389.

Date: (30 May 1908) - (Kuang-hsü 34), 5, 1.
From: Ts'ai Nai-huang, Military Intendant, Shanghai.
To: Peter Theodor Raaschou, Consul-General of Denmark,
    Shanghai.
Letter stating that the Intendant needs to know exactly in which provinces of China the Danish missionary, Miss Augusta Wied, wishes to travel before a passport can be issued.
= 2035 Konsulatsarkiver. Shanghai. Korrespondancesager m.v. 1908: nr. 72A.

390.

Date: (June) 1908.
Visiting cards from the Chinese officials in Shanghai.
= 2035 Konsulatsarkiver. Shanghai. Korrespondancesager m.v. 1908: nr. 2.

391.

Date: (3 June 1908) - (Kuang-hsü 34), 5, 5.
From: Pao Yi, Magistrate of the Mixed Court, Shanghai.
To: Wilhelm Meyer, Vice-Consul of Denmark, Shanghai.
Letter stating that the Vice-Consul is requested to write to the Great Northern Telegraph Company and ask them to summon Li Liang-ch'en, one of their employees, for the case where he is accused of having borrowed money from Lin Ken-hsien and still has not paid his debt. (Incomplete).
= 2035 Konsulatsarkiver. Shanghai. Korrespondancesager m.v. 1908: nr. 151.

392.

Date: (4 June 1908) - (Kuang-hsü 34), 5, 6.
From: The Sub-Prefect, Chefoo.
To: C.P. Kristy, Vice-Consul of Denmark, Chefoo.
Letter stating that referring to the case in which T'ang Feng-kang, a servant employed by Mr. Schwensen, an employee of the Great Northern Telegraph Company, is accused of having stolen some money etc. from the house, the Chinese authorities have now released T'ang Feng-kang on account of the lack of evidence.
= 867 Konsulatsarkiver. Chefoo 1894-1912: nr. 7.

393.

Date: (12 June 1908) - Kuang-hsü 34, 5, 14.
Petition from the Danish firm Hillebrandt and Co. requesting that the charge against the owner of the Chinese firm "Heng-sheng" can be withdrawn, as the two parties have reached a peaceful settlement of the dispute.
= 2035 Konsulatsarkiver. Shanghai. Korrespondancesager m.v. 1908: nr. 72C.

394.

Date: (13 June 1908) - Kuang-hsü 34, 5, 15.
From: Nieh Tsung-hsi, Sub-prefect of the French Mixed Court, Shanghai.
To: Peter Theodor Raaschou, Consul-General of Denmark, Shanghai.
Communication notifying the Consul of the appointment of Nieh Tsung-hsi to the post as Acting Sub-prefect of the Coast-defence of Sungchiang and Shanghai.
= 2035 Konsulatsarkiver. Shanghai. Korrespondancesager m.v. 1908: L. nr. 27.

395.

Date: (17 June 1908) - (Kuang-hsü 34), 5, 19.
From: Pao Yi, Magistrate of the Mixed Court, Shanghai.
To: Peter Theodor Raaschou, Consul-General of Denmark, Shanghai.
Letter stating that the owner of the Chinese firm "Pao-hung" Wang Hsing-ch'ing, who is sued by the Danish firm Hillebrandt and Co., has also been sued by an English business firm and has subsequently been arrested.
= 2035 Konsulatsarkiver. Shanghai. Korrespondancesager m.v. 1908: nr. 72B.

396.

Date: (18 June 1908) - (Kuang-hsü 34), 5, 20.
From: Pao Yi, Magistrate of the Mixed Court, Shanghai.
To: Peter Theodor Raaschou, Consul-General of Denmark,
   Shanghai.
Letter stating that with reference to the case Hillebrandt and Co. vs. Huang Mao-chi, the Magistrate has sent a summons to Huang Mao-chi, who has unfortunately left Shanghai and gone to Nanking.
= 2035 Konsulatsarkiver. Shanghai. Korrespondancesager m.v. 1908: nr. 55A.

397.

Date: (18 June 1908) - (Kuang-hsü 34), 5, 20.
From: Nieh Tsung-hsi, Sub-prefect of the French Mixed Court,
   Shanghai.
To: Peter Theodor Raaschou, Consul-General of Denmark,
   Shanghai.
Letter stating that on account of the appointment of Nieh-Tsung-hsi to the post of Acting Sub-prefect of Coast-defence at Sungchiang and Shanghai concurrently with his present post, he will visit the Consulate on the 20th inst.
= 2035 Konsulatsarkiver. Shanghai. Korrespondancesager m.v. 1908: L. nr. 28.

398.

Date: (20 June 1908) - Kuang-hsü 34, 5, 22.
From: Ts'ai Nai-huang, Military Intendant, Shanghai.
To: Peter Theodor Raaschou, Consul-General of Denmark,
   Shanghai.
Communication stating that Ts'ai Nai-huang is to travel to Nanking on official business.
= 2035 Konsulatsarkiver. Shanghai. Korrespondancesager m.v. 1908: L. nr. 30.

399.

Date: (22 June 1908) - Kuang-hsü 34, 5, 24.
From: Ts'ai Nai-huang, Military Intendant, Shanghai.
To: Peter Theodor Raaschou, Consul-General of Denmark,
   Shanghai.
Communication stating that Ts'ai Nai-huang has returned from a trip to Nanking on official business.
= 2035 Konsulatsarkiver. Shanghai. Korrespondancesager m.v. 1908: L. nr. 29.

400.

Date: (July 1908) - Kuang-hsü 34.
Three printed proclamations on the new Regulations for Importation of Arms and Ammunition.
= 2035 Konsulatsarkiver. Shanghai. Korrespondancesager m.v. 1908: nr. 176.

401.

Date: (July 1908) - Kuang-hsü 34, 6, -.
Petition from the Danish firm Hillebrandt and Co. requesting that Chang Mao-chang, the defendant from one of the Chinese firms "Fu-ch'an" and "Chen-ch'ang-lung", be released temporarily from prison.
= 2035 Konsulatsarkiver. Shanghai. Korrespondancesager m.v. 1908: nr. 66A.

402.

Date: (July 1908) - Kuang-hsü 34, 6, -.
Petition from the Danish firm Hillebrandt and Co. requesting that Li Hsing-tung, the defendant from one of the Chinese firms "Fu-ch'an" and "Chen-ch'ang-lung", be released temporarily from prison.
= 2035 Konsulatsarkiver. Shanghai. Korrespondancesager m.v. 1908: nr. 66B.

403.

Date: (1 July 1908) - Kuang-hsü 34, 6, 3.
Two copies of a printed notification from the Imperial Maritime Customs concerning the Regulations for Importation of Arms and Ammunition.
= 2035 Konsulatsarkiver. Shanghai. Korrespondancesager m.v. 1907: nr. 33.

404.

Date: (7 July 1908) - (Kuang-hsü 34) 6, 9.
From: Pao Yi, Magistrate of the Mixed Court, Shanghai.
To: Peter Theodor Raaschou, Consul-General of Denmark, Shanghai.
Letter stating that with reference to the case Hillebrandt and Co. vs. Huang Mao-chi, the defendant has escaped the first summons. Subsequently a new summons has been issued.
= 2035 Konsulatsarkiver. Shanghai. Korrespondancesager m.v. 1908: nr. 55B.

405.

Date: 13 July 1908 - (Kuang-hsü 34), 6, 15.
From: Ts'ai Nai-huang, Military Intendant, Shanghai.
To: Peter Theodor Raaschou, Consul-General of Denmark,
    Shanghai.
Letter stating that Ts'ai Nai-huang will receive visits and congratulations on the birthday of the Kuang-hsü Emperor, the 24th of July.
= 2035 Konsulatsarkiver. Shanghai. Korrespondancesager m.v. 1908: L. nr. 31.

406.

Date: (3 August 1908) - Kuang-hsü 34, 7, 7.
From: Tseng Yün, Governor of Chekiang.
To: Peter Theodor Raaschou, Consul-General of Denmark,
    Shanghai.
Communication notifying the Consul of the appointment of Tseng Yün to the post of Governor of Chekiang province.
= 2035 Konsulatsarkiver. Shanghai. Korrespondancesager m.v. 1908: L. nr. 32.

407.

Date: (15 August 1908) - Kuang-hsü 34, 7, 19.
From: Ts'ai Nai-huang, Military Intendant, Shanghai.
To: Peter Theodor Raaschou, Consul-General of Denmark,
    Shanghai.
Communication stating that Ts'ai Nai-huang is to travel to Nanking on official business.
= 2035 Konsulatsarkiver. Shanghai. Korrespondancesager m.v. 1908: L. nr. 33.

408.

Date: (19 August 1908) - Kuang-hsü 34, 7, 23.
From: Ts'ai Nai-huang, Military Intendant, Shanghai.
To: Peter Theodor Raaschou, Consul-General of Denmark,
    Shanghai.
Communication stating that Ts'ai Nai-huang has returned from a trip to Nanking on official business.
= 2035 Konsulatsarkiver. Shanghai. Korrespondancesager m.v. 1908: L. nr. 34.

409.

Date: (21 August 1908) - Kuang-hsü 34, 7, 25.
Printed obituary notice announcing the death of Tuan Chin, the wife of the uncle of Governor-General Tuan-Fang.
= 2035 Konsulatsarkiver. Shanghai. Korrespondancesager m.v. 1908: L. nr. 35.

410.

Date: (19 September 1908) - Kuang-hsü 34, 8, 24.
From: Ts'ai Nai-huang, Military Intendant, Shanghai.
To: Peter Theodor Raaschou, Consul-General of Denmark.
Communication stating that Ts'ai Nai-huang is to travel to Nanking on official business.
= 2035 Konsulatsarkiver. Shanghai. Korrespondancesager m.v. 1908: L. nr. 38.

411.

Date: (24 September 1908) - Kuang-hsü 34, 8, 29.
From: Ts'ai Nai-huang, Military Intendant, Shanghai.
To: Peter Theodor Raaschou, Consul-General of Denmark, Shanghai.
Communication stating that Ts'ai Nai-huang has returned from a trip to Nanking on official business.
= 2035 Konsulatsarkiver. Shanghai. Korrespondancesager m.v. 1908: L. nr. 39.

412.

Date: 26 September 1908 - (Kuang-hsü 34), 9, 2.
From: Pao Yi, Magistrate of the Mixed Court, Shanghai.
To: Peter Theodor Raaschou, Consul-General of Denmark, Shanghai.
Letter stating that the Magistrate has issued summons for Liang Hsien-ch'en, who should appear as a witness in the case between the Danish firm Hillebrandt and Co. and the Chinese merchant Chi Chi.
= 2035 Konsulatsarkiver. Shanghai. Korrespondancesager m.v. 1908: nr. 102.

413.

Date: 29 September 1908 - (Kuang-hsü 34), 9, 5.
From: Pao Yi, Magistrate of the Mixed Court, Shanghai.
To: Peter Theodor Raaschou, Consul-General of Denmark, Shanghai.
Letter stating that Magistrate Pao Yi intends to visit the Danish Consulate at half past two on the 30th inst. to discuss the case of Hillebrandt and Co. vs. T'ang He-lou, the owner of the "Pao-hung" business firm.
= 2035 Konsulatsarkiver. Shanghai. Korrespondancesager m.v. 1908: nr. 72E.

414.

Date: (1 October 1908).
From: Ts'ai Nai-huang, Military Intendant, Shanghai.
To: Peter Theodor Raaschou, Consul-General of Denmark,
    Shanghai.
Letter stating that today the Intendant will receive visits and congratulations on the birthday of the Empress Dowager.
= 2035 Konsulatsarkiver. Shanghai. Korrespondancesager m.v. 1908: L. nr. 50.

415.

Date: (14 October 1908) - (Kuang-hsü 34), 9, 20.
From: Wang Hsieh, Acting Military Intendant, Shanghai.
To: Peter Theodor Raaschou, Consul-General of Denmark,
    Shanghai.
Letter stating that on account of his appointment to the post as Acting Military Intendant of Shanghai, Wang Hsieh intends to visit the Danish Consulate on the 18th.
= 2035 Konsulatsarkiver. Shanghai. Korrespondancesager m.v. 1908: L. nr. 46.

416.

Date: (25 October 1908) - Kuang-hsü 34, 10, 1.
From: Ts'ai Nai-huang, Military Intendant, Shanghai.
To: Peter Theodor Raaschou, Consul-General of Denmark,
    Shanghai.
Communication stating that Ts'ai Nai-huang is to travel to Nanking on official business.
= 2035 Konsulatsarkiver. Shanghai. Korrespondancesager m.v. 1908: L. nr. 46.

417.

Date: (28 October 1908) - Kuang-hsü 34, 10, 4.
From: Ts'ai Nai-huang, Military Intendant, Shanghai.
To: Peter Theodor Raaschou, Consul-General of Denmark,
    Shanghai.
Communication stating that Ts'ai Nai-huang has returned from a trip to Nanking on official business.
= 2035 Konsulatsarkiver. Shanghai. Korrespondancesager m.v. 1908: L. nr. 49.

418.

Date: (31 October 1908) - (Kuang-hsü 34), 10, 7.
From: Ts'ai Nai-huang, Military Intendant, Shanghai.
To: Peter Theodor Raaschou, Consul-General of Denmark,
    Shanghai.
Letter stating that the four sporting guns can be imported by the Danish firm H. Wessel according to paragraph 4, section 3, of the new Regulations for Importation of Arms and Ammunition.
= 2035 Konsulatsarkiver. Shanghai. Korrespondancesager m.v. 1908: nr. 183.

419.

Date: (17 November 1908) - (Kuang-hsü 34), 10, 24.
From: Pao Yi, Magistrate of the Mixed Court, Shanghai.
To: Wilhelm Meyer, Vice-Consul of Denmark, Shanghai.
Letter stating that news of the death of the Empress Dowager Tz'u-hsi has been transmitted from higher authorities. In addition, notifying the Consul that the official business of the Mixed Court will be stopped for a period of 27 days.
= 2035 Konsulatsarkiver. Shanghai. Korrespondancesager m.v. 1908: L. nr. 53B.

420.

Date: (18 November 1908) - Kuang-hsü 34, 10, 25.
From: Ts'ai Nai-huang, Military Intendant, Shanghai.
To: Peter Theodor Raaschou, Consul-General of Denmark, Shanghai.
Communication stating that on account of the mourning over the death of the Empress Dowager and the Kuang-hsü Emperor, the Intendant's office will use a blue stamp in place of the usual red stamp for all official correspondence for a period of 27 days.
= 2035 Konsulatsarkiver. Shanghai. Korrespondancesager m.v. 1908: L. nr. 52.

421.

Date: (21 November 1908) - (Kuang-hsü 34), 10, 27.
From: Pao Yi, Magistrate of the Mixed Court, Shanghai.
To: Peter Theodor Raaschou, Consul-General of Denmark, Shanghai.
Letter stating that the Magistrate Pao Yi has received instructions from the Intendant notifying the Magistrate that the Empress Dowager has died on account of an illness which was aggravated by the grief she felt over the death of the Kuang-hsü Emperor.
= 2035 Konsulatsarkiver. Shanghai. Korrespondancesager m.v. 1908: L. nr. 53A.

422.

Date: (December 1908).
Copy of a petition from a Chinese merchant Li Chi-fu, stating that he has deposited a sum of tls. 500 with Mr. H. Goertz, a Danish subject who is director of the North China Coal Company, as a security for the time when Li Chi-fu was comprador of the firm. The money had not been repaid when Li Chi-fu withdrew from the firm and the Consul is requested to secure a repayment from Mr. Goertz.
= 2035 Konsulatsarkiver. Shanghai. Korrespondancesager m.v. 1908: nr. 232.

423.

Date: (2 December 1908) - Kuang-hsü 34, 11, 9.
From: Ts'ai Nai-huang, Military Intendant, Shanghai.
To: Peter Theodor Raaschou, Consul-General of Denmark, Shanghai.
Communication stating that the new Emperor of China, the Hsüan-t'ung Emperor, will ascend the throne at noon today, the 2nd of December 1908.
= 2035 Konsulatsarkiver. Shanghai. Korrespondancesager m.v. 1908: L. nr. 55.

424.

Date: (3 December 1908) - Kuang-hsü 34, 11, 10.
From: Ts'ai Nai-huang, Military Intendant, Shanghai.
To: Peter Theodor Raaschou, Consul-General of Denmark, Shanghai.
Communication stating that Ts'ai Nai-huang is to travel to Nanking on official business.
= 2035 Konsulatsarkiver. Shanghai. Korrespondancesager m.v. 1908: L. nr. 54.

425.

Date: (7 December 1908) - Kuang-hsü 34, 11, 14.
From: Ts'ai Nai-huang, Military Intendant, Shanghai.
To: Peter Theodor Raaschou, Consul-General of Denmark, Shanghai.
Communication stating that Ts'ai Nai-huang has returned to his office from a trip to Nanking on official business.
= 2035 Konsulatsarkiver. Shanghai. Korrespondancesager m.v. 1908: L. nr. 56.

426.

Date: (7 December 1908) - (Kuang-hsü 34), 11, 14.
From: Ts'ai Nai-huang, Military Intendant, Shanghai.
To: Peter Theodor Raaschou, Consul-General of Denmark, Shanghai.
Letter stating that the Danish firm is granted permission to re-export the toy air-guns imported in June-August 1907 to other places in China. Nevertheless, permission to import these air-guns to those places is part of the jurisdiction of the Intendants there and not the responsibility of Ts'ai Nai-huang.
= 2035 Konsulatsarkiver. Shanghai. Korrespondancesager m.v. 1908: nr. 212.

427.

Date: (16 December 1908) - Kuang-hsü 34, 11, 23.
From: Ts'ai Nai-huang, Military Intendant, Shanghai.
To: Peter Theodor Raaschou, Consul-General of Denmark, Shanghai.
Communication stating that the reign title of the new Emperor of China will be Hsüan-t'ung.
= 2035 Konsulatsarkiver. Shanghai. Korrespondancesager m.v. 1908: L. nr. 59.

428.

Date: (3 January 1909) - Kuang-hsü 34, 12, 12.
From: Ts'ai Nai-huang, Military Intendant, Shanghai.
To: Peter Theodor Raaschou, Consul-General of Denmark, Shanghai.
Communication stating that Ts'ai Nai-huang is to travel to Nanking on official business.
= 2035 Konsulatsarkiver. Shanghai. Korrespondancesager m.v. 1909: L. nr. 1.

429.

Date: (7 January 1909) - Kuang-hsü 34, 12, 16.
From: Ts'ai Nai-huang, Military Intendant, Shanghai.
To: Peter Theodor Raaschou, Consul-General of Denmark, Shanghai.
Communication stating that Ts'ai Nai-huang has returned from a trip to Nanking on official business.
= 2035 Konsulatsarkiver. Shanghai. Korrespondancesager m.v. 1909: L. nr. 3.

430.

Date: (31 January 1909) - (Hsüan-t'ung 1), 1, 10.
From: Ts'ai Nai-huang, Military Intendant, Shanghai.
To: Peter Theodor Raaschou, Consul-General of Denmark, Shanghai.
Letter stating that the Superintendant of Trade at the Southern Ports Tuan-Fang will receive the participants at the Meeting on Prohibition of Opium Smoking on the 2nd of February in his office. The Consul is requested to send a representative of his country to the meeting.
= 2035 Konsulatsarkiver. Shanghai. Korrespondancesager m.v. 1909: L. nr. 2.

431.

Date: (February 1909) - Hsüan-t'ung 1, 1, -.
Petition from the Danish firm W. Funder and Co. stating that a Chinese clerk, Cheng Hsü-po, has committed theft and swindling while he was employed in the firm. The firm requests that the Mixed Court arrest and punish Cheng Hsü-po and order his father Cheng Kan-t'ing to pay back the losses caused by his son to the firm.
= 2035 Konsulatsarkiver. Shanghai. Korrespondancesager m.v. 1909: nr. 17A.

432.

Date: (3 February 1909) - Hsüan-t'ung 1, 1, 13.
Passport for a trip to Russia for the Chinese merchant Chen Pao-yung, a comprador of the Danish firm Andersen, Meyer and Co.
= 2035 Konsulatsarkiver. Shanghai. Korrespondancesager m.v. 1909: nr. 11.

433.

Date: (19 February 1909) - (Hsüan-t'ung 1), 1, 29.
From: Pao Yi, Magistrate of the Mixed Court, Shanghai.
To: Peter Theodor Raaschou, Consul-General of Denmark, Shanghai.
Letter stating that a letter has been received from the Consul with a petition from the Danish firm W. Funder and Co. asking for the arrest of Cheng Kan-t'ing and his son for theft. The Magistrate has issued a summons for the defendants.
= 2035 Konsulatsarkiver. Shanghai. Korrespondancesager m.v. 1909: nr. 17B.

434.

Date: (1 March 1909) - (Hsüan-t'ung 1), 2, 10.
From: Pao Yi, Magistrate of the Mixed Court, Shanghai.
To: Peter Theodor Raaschou, Consul-General of Denmark, Shanghai.
Letter stating that the Danish firm Andersen, Meyer and Co. has requested that the Mixed Court close down the houses on the property of the firm on the Ningpo Road and enforce payment of the rent. The Magistrate has sent runners to close the houses.
= 2035 Konsulatsarkiver. Shanghai. Korrespondancesager m.v. 1909: nr. 24.

435.

Date: (8 March 1909) - Hsüan-t'ung 1, 2, 17.
From: Ts'ai Nai-huang, Military Intendant, Shanghai.
To: Peter Theodor Raaschou, Consul-General of Denmark, Shanghai.
Communication stating that Ts'ai Nai-huang has returned from a trip to Nanking on official business.
= 2035 Konsulatsarkiver. Shanghai. Korrespondancesager m.v. 1909: L. nr. 4.

436.

Date: (19 March 1909) - (Hsüan-t'ung 1, 2, 28).
Obituary notice for Madam Hsia, Mother of Wan Chung-an and Wan Chung-yüan. The funeral will take place on the 22nd of April.
= 2035 Konsulatsarkiver. Shanghai. Korrespondancesager m.v. 1909: L. nr. 5.

437.

Date: (28 March 1909) - (Hsüan-t'ung 1), Jun2, 7.
Printed edition of the Laws for Registration of National Subjects.
Contents:
Memorial from the Constitutional Government Committee for Investigation of Registration.
Laws for Registration of National Subjects.
Regulations for the application of the Laws.
Six Registration Forms.
= 2035 Konsulatsarkiver. Shanghai. Korrespondancesager m.v. 1910: nr. 71.

438.

Date: (11 May 1909) - (Hsüan-t'ung 1), 3, 22.
From: Ts'ai Nai-huang, Military Intendant, Shanghai.
To: Peter Theodor Raaschou, Consul-General of Denmark, Shanghai.
Letter stating that the Superintendent of Trade at the Southern Ports, Tuan-Fang, wishes to thank the Consul-General of Denmark, Peter Theodor Raaschou, for flying the flag at half mast on the 1st of May when the funeral for the late Kuang-hsü Emperor took place.
= 2035 Konsulatsarkiver. Shanghai. Korrespondancesager m.v. 1909: L. nr. 6.

439.

Date: (21 May) 1908 - (Kuang-hsü 34), 4, 22.
From: The Sub-Prefect, Chefoo.
To: C.P. Kristy, Vice-Consul of Denmark, Chefoo.
Letter stating that the servant T'ang Feng-kang has given the statement that he never had the opportunity to steal from Mr. Schwensen. He has never had a key to the house. The Chinese authorities believe that he is lying but the case cannot be solved immediately unless more information can be obtained regarding exactly when the things were stolen etc.
= 867 Konsulatsarkiver. Chefoo. 1894-1912: nr. 9.

440.

Date: (31 May 1909) - (Hsüan-t'ung 1), 4, 13.
From: Sheng Hsüan-huai, Nanking.
To: Peter Theodor Raaschou, Consul-General of Denmark, Shanghai.
Letter in reply stating that Sheng Hsüan-huai is sorry to say that he cannot visit the Consulate on the 3rd of July to congratulate him on the birthday of the Danish King, because he is unable to wear his official cap on account of a headache created by the moist climate.
= 2035 Konsulatsarkiver. Shanghai. Korrespondancesager m.v. 1909: L. nr. 7.

441.

Date: (31 May 1909) - (Hsüan-t'ung 1), 4, 13.
From: Ts'ai Nai-huang, Military Intendant, Shanghai.
To: Peter Theodor Raaschou, Consul-General of Denmark, Shanghai.
Letter stating that Ts'ai Nai-huang is presently suffering from a slight indisposition. If it passes over before the 3rd of July, the Intendant will visit the Consulate to offer his congratulations on the birthday of the Danish King. If he is not well at that time, he will send a representative of his office.
= 2035 Konsulatsarkiver. Shanghai. Korrespondancesager m.v. 1909: L. nr. 8.

442.

Date: (June 1909) - Hsüan-t'ung 1, 5, -.
Petition from the Danish firm W. Funder requesting the Mixed Court to enforce the payment of tls. 105.04 from the Chinese merchant Lao Wang.
= 2035 Konsulatsarkiver. Shanghai. Korrespondancesager m.v. 1909: nr. 71B.

443.

Date: (June 1909) - Hsüan-t'ung 1, 5, -.
Petition from the Danish firm W. Funder and Co.
requesting that the Mixed Court enforce the payment of
losses amounting to tls. 241.53 from the Chinese
merchant Ch'en Yü-ch'ing, owner of the "Sen-t'ai" shop.
= 2035 Konsulatsarkiver. Shanghai. Korrespondancesager
m.v. 1909: nr. 71C.

444.

Date: (June 1909) - Hsüan-t'ung 1, 5, -.
Petition from the Danish firm W. Funder and Co.
requesting that the Mixed Court enforce payment of
tls. 100.88 from the Chinese merchant Jung Chi.
= 2035 Konsulatsarkiver. Shanghai. Korrespondancesager
m.v. 1909: nr. 71D.

445.

Date: 24 June 1909 - Hsüan-t'ung 1, 5, 7.
From: Ts'ai Nai-huang, Military Intendant, Shanghai.
To: T. Hansen, Acting Consul of Denmark, Shanghai.
Communication stating that Ts'ai Nai-huang is to travel
to Nanking on official business.
= 2035 Konsulatsarkiver. Shanghai. Korrespondancesager
m.v. 1909: L. nr. 9.

446.

Date: (29 June 1909) - Hsüan-t'ung 1, 5, 12.
From: Ts'ai Nai-huang, Military Intendant, Shanghai.
To: T. Hansen, Acting Consul of Denmark, Shanghai.
Communication stating that Ts'ai Nai-huang has returned
from a trip to Nanking on official business.
= 2035 Konsulatsarkiver. Shanghai. Korrespondancesager
m.v. 1909: L. nr. 10.

447.

Date: (9 July 1909) - Hsüan-t'ung 1, 5, 22.
From: Ts'ai Nai-huang, Military Intendant, Shanghai.
To: T. Hansen, Acting Consul of Denmark, Shanghai.
Communication stating that Ts'ai Nai-huang is to travel
to Nanking on official business.
= 2035 Konsulatsarkiver. Shanghai. Korrespondancesager
m.v. 1909: L. nr. 11.

448.

Date: (18 July 1909) - (Hsüan-t'ung 1), 6, 2.
From: Ts'ai Nai-huang, Military Intendant, Shanghai.
To: Peter Theodor Raaschou, Consul-General of Denmark, Shanghai.
Letter stating that the Intendant has been instructed by the Superintendant of Trade at the Southern Ports, Tuan-Fang, to forward a copy of a telegram concerning the absence from the post of Tuan-Fang.
Appended: A copy of the telegram stating that Tuan-Fang is leaving for Peking on official business.
= 2035 Konsulatsarkiver. Shanghai. Korrespondancesager m.v. 1909: L. nr. 12.

449.

Date: (22 July 1909) - Hsüan-t'ung 1, 6, 8.
From: Ts'ai Nai-huang, Military Intendant, Shanghai.
To: T. Hansen, Acting Consul of Denmark, Shanghai.
Communication stating that a telegram has been received from the Superintendant of Trade at the Southern Ports, Tuan-Fang, notifying the Consul that he has been appointed to the post as Governor-General of Chihli province. His duties are subsequently transferred to Acting Superintendant Fan Tseng-hsiang.
= 2035 Konsulatsarkiver. Shanghai. Korrespondancesager m.v. 1909: L. nr. 13.

450.

Date: (1 August 1909) - Hsüan-t'ung 1, 6, 16.
From: Ts'ai Nai-huang, Military Intendant, Shanghai.
To: T. Hansen, Acting Consul of Denmark, Shanghai.
Communication notifying the Consul of the appointment of Fan Tseng-hsiang to the post as Acting Superintendant of Trade at the Southern Ports.
= 2035 Konsulatsarkiver. Shanghai. Korrespondancesager m.v. 1909: L. nr. 14.

451.

Date: (24 August 1909) - Hsüan-t'ung 1, 7, 9.
From: Ts'ai Nai-huang, Military Intendant, Shanghai.
To: T. Hansen, Consul of Denmark, Shanghai.
Communication stating that Ts'ai Nai-huang is to travel to Nanking on official business.
= 2035 Konsulatsarkiver. Shanghai. Korrespondancesager m.v. 1909: L. nr. 15.

452.

Date: (27 August 1909) - (Hsüan-t'ung 1), 7, 12.
From: Ts'ai Nai-huang, Military Intendant, Shanghai.
To: Peter Theodor Raaschou, Consul-General of Denmark, Shanghai.
Letter stating that the Consul should instruct his subjects that they should not render any support to the "Shen-chou"-newspaper bureau, because it is managed solely on a Chinese basis.
= 2035 Konsulatsarkiver. Shanghai. Korrespondancesager m.v. 1909: L. nr. 16.

453.

Date: (29 August 1909) - Hsüan-t'ung 1, 7, 14.
From: Ts'ai Nai-huang, Military Intendant, Shanghai.
To: T. Hansen, Consul of Denmark, Shanghai.
Communication stating that Ts'ai Nai-huang has returned from a trip to Nanking on official business.
= 2035 Konsulatsarkiver. Shanghai. Korrespondancesager m.v. 1909: L. nr. 17.

454.

Date: (1 September 1909) - (Hsüan-t'ung 1), 7, 17.
From: Ts'ai Nai-huang, Military Intendant, Shanghai.
To: T. Hansen, Consul of Denmark, Shanghai.
Communication notifying the Consul that the new Superintendant of Trade at the Southern Ports, Chang Jen-chün, has arrived in Nanking and is taking over the post from Acting Superintendant Fan Ts'eng-hsiang.
= 2035 Konsulatsarkiver. Shanghai. Korrespondancesager m.v. 1909: L. nr. 18.

455.

Date: (29 October 1909) - (Hsüan-t'ung 1), 9, 16.
From: Pao Yi, Magistrate of the Mixed Court, Shanghai.
To: T. Hansen, Consul of Denmark, Shanghai.
Letter stating that the Magistrate Pao Yi has summoned all the defendants in the case W. Funder and Co. vs. Jung Chi and the "Sen-t'ai" shop.
= 2035 Konsulatsarkiver. Shanghai. Korrespondancesager m.v. 1909: nr. 71E.

456.

Date: (5 November 1909) - (Hsüan-t'ung 1), 9, 23.
From: Pao Yi, Magistrate of the Mixed Court, Shanghai.
To: T. Hansen, Consul of Denmark, Shanghai.
Letter stating that the Magistrate Pao Yi has issued summons for the defendants in the case East Asiatic Company vs. the "Chih-hsing-ch'ang-chi" company.
= 2035 Konsulatsarkiver. Shanghai. Korrespondancesager m.v. 1909: nr. 97A.

457.

Date: (8 November 1909) - (Hsüan-t'ung 1), 9, 26.
From: Pao Yi, Magistrate of the Mixed Court, Shanghai.
To: T. Hansen, Consul of Denmark, Shanghai.
Letter stating that the case W. Funder vs. Ch'en Yü-ch'ing will be heard on the 10th inst. The Consul is requested to attend with the plaintiff.
= 2035 Konsulatsarkiver. Shanghai. Korrespondancesager m.v. 1909: nr. 71A.

458.

Date: (10 November 1909) - (Hsüan-t'ung 1), 9, 28.
From: Ts'ai Nai-huang, Military Intendant, Shanghai.
To: Peter Theodor Raaschou, Consul-General of Denmark, Shanghai.
Letter stating that the illegal "Sigh of the People Daily" (Min-yü-jih-pao) has been distributed in Shanghai from Japan by a French merchant. The French Consul-General has stated that the said merchant has ceased distribution on the 7th inst. The Consul is requested to warn his subjects against involvement in distribution of illegal papers.
= 2035 Konsulatsarkiver. Shanghai. Korrespondancesager m.v. 1909: nr. 104.

459.

Date: (17 November 1909) - (Hsüan-t'ung 1), 10, 5.
From: Pao Yi, Magistrate of the Mixed Court, Shanghai.
To: T. Hansen, Consul of Denmark, Shanghai.
Letter stating that the Chinese firm "Chih-hsing-ch'ang-chi", which has been sued by the Danish firm East Asiatic Company, has not been sued by an American business firm, as was stated by the Consul in his letter.
= 2035 Konsulatsarkiver. Shanghai. Korrespondancesager m.v. 1909: nr. 97B.

460.

Date: (22 November 1909) - (Hsüan-t'ung 1), 10, 10.
From: Pao Yi, Magistrate of the Mixed Court, Shanghai.
To: T. Hansen, Consul of Denmark, Shanghai.
Letter stating that the Magistrate has summoned the defendant in the case W. Funder vs. Ch'en Yü-ch'ing, owner of the "Sen-t'ai" shop.
= 2035 Konsulatsarkiver. Shanghai. Korrespondancesager m.v. 1909: nr. 71F.

461.

Date: (16 December 1909) - (Hsüan-t'ung 1), 11, 4.
From: Pao Yi, Magistrate of the Mixed Court, Shanghai.
To: Peter Theodor Raaschou, Consul-General of Denmark,
    Shanghai.
Letter stating that the Mixed Court would like to establish the procedure in law-suits between foreign and Chinese subjects that the foreign plaintiffs should send petitions to the Mixed Court in both Chinese and English. Thereby the confusion on the part of the defendants as to what they are accused of is avoided.
= 2035 Konsulatsarkiver. Shanghai. Korrespondancesager m.v. 1909: nr. 127.

462.

Date: (1910).
From: Hu T'iao-yüan, Magistrate of the Pao-shan district.
To: Peter Theodor Raaschou, Consul-General of Denmark,
    Shanghai.
Letter stating that Ku Po-hua has left his post at the Land Surveying Office in the Pao-shan district. Liu Yi-yün takes over.
= 2035 Konsulatsarkiver. Shanghai. Korrespondancesager m.v. 1910: nr. 72.

463.

Date: (4 January 1910) - (Hsüan-t'ung 1), 11, 23.
From: Ts'ai Nai-huang, Military Intendant, Shanghai.
To: Peter Theodor Raaschou, Consul-General of Denmark,
    Shanghai.
Letter requesting the Consul to forward information on the Churches built by Danish missionaries in the districts of Shanghai and Pao-shan, and the names and addresses of Danish missionaries in these districts.
= 2035 Konsulatsarkiver. Shanghai. Korrespondancesager m.v. 1910: nr. 3.

464.

Date: (7 January 1910) - (Hsüan-t'ung 1), 11, 26.
From: Pao Yi, Magistrate of the Mixed Court, Shanghai.
To: Peter Theodor Raaschou, Consul-General of Denmark,
    Shanghai.
Letter stating that orders have been received from the Intendant stating that the defendant in the case of Shen Yüan-fu vs. Ts'ao Chi-an, a Chinese subject employed by a German firm, should be sent to the City Magistrate of the Chinese Settlement for trial, as the case is solely concerned with Chinese subjects. In addition, the Intendant has suggested that the Consul should stamp warrants for the Chinese subjects sued by a foreign firm officially.
= 2035 Konsulatsarkiver. Shanghai. Korrespondancesager m.v. 1909: L. nr. 19.

465.

Date: (15 January 1910) - (Hsüan-t'ung 1), 12, 5.
From: Pao Yi, Magistrate of the Mixed Court, Shanghai.
To: T. Hansen, Consul of Denmark, Shanghai.
Letter stating that a judgement has been passed in the case of W. Funder vs. Ch'en Yü-ch'ing.
Appended: The judgement in the case, namely that Ch'en Yü-ch'ing should pay the loss of tls. 31.55 to W. Funder within two weeks.
= 2035 Konsulatsarkiver. Shanghai. Korrespondancesager m.v. 1909: nr. 71G.

466.

Date: (17 January 1910) - (Hsüan-t'ung 1), 12, 7.
From: Ts'ai Nai-huang, Military Intendant, Shanghai.
To: Peter Theodor Raaschou, Consul-General of Denmark, Shanghai.
Letter stating that five Japanese students have ignored an official order not to travel through the Miao-chiang and Yao-t'ung areas in Kweichow province, and subsequently had to be brought out of these areas under military protection. Foreigners are warned not to travel in these areas where the local population is a savage people.
= 2035 Konsulatsarkiver. Shanghai. Korrespondancesager m.v. 1910: nr. 15.

467.

Date: (25 January 1910) - (Hsüan-t'ung 1), 12, 15.
From: Ts'ai Nai-huang, Military Intendant, Shanghai.
To: Peter Theodor Raaschou, Consul-General of Denmark, Shanghai.
Letter requesting the Consul to forward information on the Danish subjects living in the Pao-shan district.
Appended: Two blank forms for registration of households, persons, etc. in the Pao-shan district.
= 2035 Konsulatsarkiver. Shanghai. Korrespondancesager m.v. 1910: nr. 21.

468.

Date: (5 February 1910) - (Hsüan-t'ung 1), 12, 26.
From: Hu T'iao-yüan, Magistrate of the Pao-shan district.
To: Peter Theodor Raaschou, Consul-General of Denmark, Shanghai.
Letter requesting the Consul to forward information on the Danish firms that have rented land in the Pao-shan district. The land-tax for the year 1910, 2000 cash per mou, is due to be paid now.
= 2035 Konsulatsarkiver. Shanghai. Korrespondancesager m.v. 1910: nr. 20A.

469.

Date: (6 February 1910) - (Hsüan-t'ung 1), 12, 27.
From: Peter Theodor Raaschou, Consul-General of Denmark,
    Shanghai.
To: Hu T'iao-yüan, Magistrate of the Pao-shan district.
Copy of a letter stating that the Great Northern
Telegraph Company has rented a strip of land in the
Pao-shan district, and giving the exact position of the
land.
= 2035 Konsulatsarkiver. Shanghai. Korrespondancesager
m.v. 1910: nr. 20B.

470.

Date: 5 March 1910 - Hsüan-t'ung 2, 1, 24.
Passport for the Danish merchant Svend Aage Magnussen
for travels in the provinces Kiangsu, Anwei, Chekiang,
Kiangsi and Honan.
= 2035 Konsulatsarkiver. Shanghai. Korrespondancesager
m.v. 1911: L. nr. 6.

471.

Date: (23 March 1910) - (Hsüan-t'ung 2), 2, 13.
From: Ts'ai Nai-huang, Military Intendant, Shanghai.
To: Peter Theodor Raaschou, Consul-General of Denmark,
    Shanghai.
Letter stating that in the past, Consuls have often
requested the Intendant to issue proclamations for
protection of their merchant's interests. Recently the
Belgian Consul wanted a proclamation against gambling in
the International Settlement of Shanghai, but later
stated in a letter to the Intendant that the police of
the International Settlement are able to keep order and
that the co-operation of the Intendant is unnecessary.
The Intendant would like to point out that the Settlement is Chinese territory and that it is his proper duty
as a Chinese official to maintain order there.
= 2035 Konsulatsarkiver. Shanghai. Korrespondancesager
m.v. 1910: nr. 55.

472.

Date: (8 April 1910) - (Hsüan-t'ung 2), 2, 29.
From: Ts'ai Nai-huang, Military Intendant, Shanghai.
To: T. Hansen, Consul of Denmark, Shanghai.
Letter stating that the Danish firm, Schiller and Co.,
can import and trans-ship to Tientsin a sporting-gun
with cartridges according to paragraph 8 of the new
Regulations on Importation of Arms and Ammunition.
= 2035 Konsulatsarkiver. Shanghai. Korrespondancesager
m.v. 1910: nr. 56.

473.

Date: (19 April 1910).
From: Ch'en Ch'i, The Bureau of the Nanyang Industrial
    Exhibition.
To: Peter Theodor Raaschou, Consul-General of Denmark,
    Shanghai.
Letter stating that Danish firms who wish to participate
in the Nanyang Industrial Exhibition should forward a
list of the goods presented at the Exhibition to the
Bureau within one week.
= 2035 Konsulatsarkiver. Shanghai. Korrespondancesager
m.v. 1909: nr. 71.

474.

Date: (24 April 1910) - (Hsüan-t'ung 2), 3, 15.
From: Ts'ai Nai-huang, Military Intendant, Shanghai.
To: Peter Theodor Raaschou, Consul-General of Denmark,
    Shanghai.
Letter stating that a copy of the Rules for Registration
of National Subjects and a book with the Laws for
Registration of National Subjects are hereby forwarded.
Appended: Rules for Registration of National Subjects.
= 2035 Konsulatsarkiver. Shanghai. Korrespondancesager
m.v. 1910: nr. 71.
(See also nr. 437 in this catalogue).

475.

Date: (27 July 1910) - Hsüan-t'ung 2, 6, 21.
From: Sheng Hsüan-huai, Minister of the Ministry of
    Posts and Communication.
To: Peter Theodor Raaschou, Consul-General of Denmark,
    Shanghai.
Communication notifying the Consul that Sheng Hsüan-huai
has been appointed President of the Department for the
Three Eastern Provinces of the Chinese Red Cross Society.
= 2035 Konsulatsarkiver. Shanghai. Korrespondancesager
m.v. 1910: L. nr. 9.

476.

Date: (22 August 1910) - (Hsüan-t'ung 2), 7, 18.
From: Liu Yen-yi, Military Intendant, Shanghai.
To: Peter Theodor Raaschou, Consul-General of Denmark,
    Shanghai.
Letter stating that a letter has been received from the
Consul requesting an import-permit for a rifle plus one
box of cartridges to be used by Count Ahlefeldt, the
Secretary of the Danish Legation in Peking, for his own
protection. The Intendant states that he has previously
granted permission to the Consul-General, stating that
he should import the rifle according to paragraph 8 of
the new Regulations on Importation of Arms and Ammunition.
= 2035 Konsulatsarkiver. Shanghai. Korrespondancesager
m.v. 1911: nr. 135.

477.

Date: (22 September 1910) - (Hsüan-t'ung 2), 8, 19.
From: Pao Yi, Magistrate of the Mixed Court, Shanghai.
To: Wilhelm Meyer, Vice-Consul of Denmark, Shanghai.
Letter stating that with reference to the liquidation of the Chinese firm "Mou ch'ang", the Consul is requested to state whether the firm Hillebrandt and Co. is Danish and whether Hillebrandt and Co. has a claim of tls. 197.20 against the "Mou-ch'ang" company.
= 2035 Konsulatsarkiver. Shanghai. Korrespondancesager m.v. 1911: nr. 150A.

478.

Date: (8 October 1910) - (Hsüan-t'ung 2), 9, 6.
From: Ts'ai Nai-huang, Military Intendant, Shanghai.
To: Peter Theodor Raaschou, Consul-General of Denmark, Shanghai.
Letter stating that the Intendant will try to settle the case of a debt of tls. 10,000 owed by T'ang Shao-k'ang to the Danish subject O. Møller by a peaceful settlement.
= 2035 Konsulatsarkiver. Shanghai. Korrespondancesager m.v. 1910: nr. 148.

479.

Date: (14 October 1910) - Hsüan-t'ung 2, 9, 12.
From: Liu Yen-yi, Military Intendant, Shanghai.
To: Peter Theodor Raaschou, Consul-General of Denmark, Shanghai.
Communication notifying the Consul that Liu Yen-yi has taken over the post of Military Intendant and Inspector of Customs at Shanghai from Ts'ai Nai-huang.
= 2035 Konsulatsarkiver. Shanghai. Korrespondancesager m.v. 1910: L. nr. 14.

480.

Date: (14 October 1910) - (Hsüan-t'ung 2), 9, 12.
From: Liu Yen-yi, Military Intendant, Shanghai.
To: Peter Theodor Raaschou, Consul-General of Denmark, Shanghai.
Letter stating that on account of the appointment of Liu Yen-yi to the post of Military Intendant and Inspector of Customs at Shanghai, he intends to visit the Danish Consulate on the 17th inst.
= 2035 Konsulatsarkiver. Shanghai. Korrespondancesager m.v. 1910: L. nr. 13.

481.

Date: (1 November 1910) - (Hsüan-t'ung 2), 9, 30.
From: Liu Yen-yi, Military Intendant, Shanghai.
To: Peter Theodor Raaschou, Consul-General of Denmark,
    Shanghai.
Letter stating that the Intendant will visit the Consulate
at 3 o'clock on the 7th inst.
= 2035 Konsulatsarkiver. Shanghai. Korrespondancesager
m.v. 1910: L. nr. 15.

482.

Date: (7 November 1910) - (Hsüan-t'ung 2), 10, 6.
From: Hu T'iao-yüan, Magistrate of the Pao-shan district.
To: Peter Theodor Raaschou, Consul-General of Denmark,
    Shanghai.
Letter stating that Liu Yi-yün, being engaged otherwise,
is unable to manage the Land Surveying Office in the
Pao-shan district. Ch'en Kuei-hsien takes over.
= 2035 Konsulatsarkiver. Shanghai. Korrespondancesager
m.v. 1910: L. nr. 16.

483.

Date: (24 November 1910) - (Hsüan-t'ung 2), 10, 23.
From: Liu Yen-yi, Military Intendant, Shanghai.
To: Peter Theodor Raaschou, Consul-General of Denmark,
    Shanghai.
Letter stating that Li Ch'ang-chün has been transferred
from his post at the Land Surveying Office in Shanghai to
a post in Tientsin. Chou Ching-fang takes over.
= 2035 Konsulatsarkiver. Shanghai. Korrespondancesager
m.v. 1910: L. nr. 17.

484.

Date: (3 December 1910) - Hsüan-t'ung 2, 11, 2.
From: Wang Chia-t'ang, Commissioner of Foreign Affairs
    in Kiangsu.
To: Peter Theodor Raaschou, Consul-General of Denmark,
    Shanghai.
Communication notifying the Consul of the appointment of
Wang Chia-t'ang to the post as Commissioner of Foreign
Affairs in Kiangsu.
= 2035 Konsulatsarkiver. Shanghai. Korrespondancesager
m.v. 1910: L. nr. 12.

485.

Date: 8 December 1910 - (Hsüan-t'ung 2), 11, 7.
From: Liu Yen-yi, Military Intendant, Shanghai.
To: Peter Theodor Raaschou, Consul-General of Denmark, Shanghai.
Letter granting the Danish firm East Asiatic Company permission to import 20 revolvers, 6000 cartridges, etc. for use by the guards at the German Legation in Peking.
= 2035 Konsulatsarkiver. Shanghai. Korrespondancesager m.v. 1910: nr. 168.

486.

Date: (28 December 1910) - (Hsüan-t'ung 2), 11, 27.
From: Hu T'iao-yüan, Magistrate of the Pao-shan district.
To: Peter Theodor Raaschou, Consul-General of Denmark, Shanghai.
Letter stating that the land tax for the year 1911, 2000 cash per mou, is due to be collected in the Pao-shan district. The Consul-General is requested to forward a list of foreigners renting land in the district.
= 2035 Konsulatsarkiver. Shanghai. Korrespondancesager m.v. 1911: nr. 5.

487.

Date: (29 December 1910) - (Hsüan-t'ung 2), 11, 28.
From: Ch'en Ch'i, The Bureau of the Nanyang Industrial Exhibition.
To: Peter Theodor Raaschou, Consul-General of Denmark, Shanghai.
Letter expressing gratitude for the help received from the Consul-General of Denmark at Shanghai, Peter Theodor Raaschou, and the Danish firm Andersen, Meyer and Co. for their participation in the Nanyang Industrial Exhibition held in Nanking in May-October 1910.
= 2035 Konsulatsarkiver. Shanghai. Korrespondancesager m.v. 1909: nr. 90B.

488.

Date: (4 January 1911) - Hsüan-t'ung 2, 12, 4.
From: Liu Yen-yi, Military Intendant, Shanghai.
To: Peter Theodor Raaschou, Consul-General of Denmark, Shanghai.
Communication stating that Liu Yen-yi is to travel to Nanking on official business.
= 2035 Konsulatsarkiver. Shanghai. Korrespondancesager m.v. 1911: L. nr. 11.

489.

Date: (9 January 1911) - Hsüan-t'ung 2, 12, 9.
From: Liu Yen-yi, Military Intendant, Shanghai.
To: Peter Theodor Raaschou, Consul-General of Denmark, Shanghai.
Communication stating that Liu Yen-yi has returned from a trip to Nanking on official business.
= 2035 Konsulatsarkiver. Shanghai. Korrespondancesager m.v. 1911: L. nr. 10.

490.

Date: (14 January 1911) - (Hsüan-t'ung 2), 12, 14.
From: Liu Yen-yi, Military Intendant, Shanghai.
To: Peter Theodor Raaschou, Consul-General of Denmark, Shanghai.
Letter stating that the passport for the Danish missionary, N. Kristiansen, has been issued by the Consul to be valid for two years. This is contrary to the usual time-limit for such passes which is only one year. The passport is returned for correction of the dates.
= 2035 Konsulatsarkiver. Shanghai. Korrespondancesager m.v. 1911: nr. 10A.

491.

Date: (21 January 1911) - (Hsüan-t'ung 2), 12, 21.
From: Liu Yen-yi, Military Intendant, Shanghai.
To: Peter Theodor Raaschou, Consul-General of Denmark, Shanghai.
Letter granting Mr. I. Andersen, a Danish subject, permission to import a pistol plus 200 cartridges to use for his own protection.
= 2035 Konsulatsarkiver. Shanghai. Korrespondancesager m.v. 1911: nr. 11.

492.

Date: 29 January 1911 - (Hsüan-t'ung 2), 12, 29.
From: Kuan Chiung, Magistrate of the Mixed Court, Shanghai.
To: Peter Theodor Raaschou, Consul-General of Denmark, Shanghai.
Letter stating that the claim of the Danish firm Hillebrandt and Co. against the Chinese firm "Mou-ch'ang" of tls. 197.20 has been managed by the previous Magistrate of the Mixed Court, Pao Yi. The Consul is requested to state the full particulars of the case for further action.
= 2035 Konsulatsarkiver. Shanghai. Korrespondancesager m.v. 1911: nr. 150B.

493.

Date: (16 March 1911) - Hsüan-t'ung 3, 2, 16.
From: Liu Yen-yi, Military Intendant, Shanghai.
To: Peter Theodor Raaschou, Consul-General of Denmark,
     Shanghai.
Communication stating that Liu Yen-yi is to travel to
Nanking on official business.
= 2035 Konsulatsarkiver. Shanghai. Korrespondancesager
m.v. 1911: L. nr. 9.

494.

Date: 20 March 1911 - (Hsüan-t'ung 3), 2, 20.
From: Wang Chia-t'ang, Commissioner of Foreign Affairs.
To: Peter Theodor Raaschou, Consul-General of Denmark,
     Shanghai.
Letter stating that Wang Chia-t'ang will visit the
Consulate on the 21st inst.
= 2035 Konsulatsarkiver. Shanghai. Korrespondancesager
m.v. 1911: L. nr. 8.

495.

Date: (22 March 1911) - Hsüan-t'ung 3, 2, 22.
From: Liu Yen-yi, Military Intendant, Shanghai.
To: Peter Theodor Raaschou, Consul-General of Denmark,
     Shanghai.
Communication stating that Liu Yen-yi has returned from
a trip to Nanking on official business.
= 2035 Konsulatsarkiver. Shanghai. Korrespondancesager
m.v. 1911: nr. 7.

496.

Date: 9 April 1911 - Hsüan-t'ung 3, 3, 11.
From: Ministry of Foreign Affairs, Peking.
To: N. Kolessoff.
Copy of a communication stating that the Ministry of
Posts and Communication has memoralized the throne
concerning the agreement with the Great Northern Telegraph
Company and the Eastern Extension Telegraph Company about
an advance of the telegraph revenues. An Imperial Edict
has been received carrying instructions to the Chinese
authorities to commence with the negotiations.
= Store Nordiske Arkiv.

497.

Date: *10 April 1911.*
Agreement between China, the Great Northern Telegraph Company and the Eastern Extension Telegraph Company concerning a loan of 500,000 pounds sterling to China.
= Store Nordiske Arkiv.

498.

Date: *11 April 1911 - Hsüan-t'ung 3, 3, 13.*
Petition from the Danish firm Andersen, Meyer and Co. requesting that the Chinese firm "Shun-feng" be instructed to pay tls. 1,865.20 and take delivery of eight boxes with Black Vicuna cloth.
= 2035 Konsulatsarkiver. Shanghai. Korrespondancesager m.v. 1911: nr. 69B.

499.

Date: *(May 1911) - Hsüan-t'ung 3, 4, -.*
Deed of property for a piece of land in Shanghai rented by the Danish subject L. Nelleman. Issued by the Chinese owners, Wu Ch'ing-an and others.
= 2035 Konsulatsarkiver. Shanghai. Korrespondancesager m.v. 1911: nr. 96A.

500.

Date: *(4 May 1911) - (Hsüan-t'ung 3), 4, 6.*
From: Pao Yi, Magistrate of the Mixed Court, Shanghai.
To: Peter Theodor Raaschou, Consul-General of Denmark, Shanghai.
Letter stating that Yang Chia-t'ang, the defendant in the case Andersen, Meyer and Co. vs. the "Shun-feng" company, has gone to Suchou on a business-trip. The Magistrate is going to send summons in order to bring him back to Shanghai.
= 2035 Konsulatsarkiver. Shanghai. Korrespondancesager m.v. 1911: nr. 69A.

501.

Date: *(21 May 1911) - (Hsüan-t'ung 3), 9, 23.*
From: Kuan Chiung, Magistrate of the Mixed Court, Shanghai.
To: Peter Theodor Raaschou, Consul-General of Denmark, Shanghai.
Letter stating that Kuan Chiung has been appointed to the post as Magistrate of the Mixed Court at Shanghai by the Intendant, Liu Yen-yi. Therefore he would like to visit the Consulate on the 22nd inst.
= 2035 Konsulatsarkiver. Shanghai. Korrespondancesager m.v. 1911: L. nr. 1.

502.

Date: 30 May 1911 (Hsüan-t'ung 3), 5, 3.
From: Liu Yen-yi, Military Intendant, Shanghai.
To: Peter Theodor Raaschou, Consul-General of Denmark, Shanghai.
Letter stating that the invitation to visit the Danish Consulate on the birthday of the Danish King is accepted.
= 2035 Konsulatsarkiver. Shanghai. Korrespondancesager m.v. 1911: nr. 5.

503.

Date: (21 June 1911) - (Hsüan-t'ung 3), 5, 25.
From: Liu Yen-yi, Military Intendant, Shanghai.
To: Peter Theodor Raaschou, Consul-General of Denmark, Shanghai.
Letter stating that the deed of property for a piece of land rented by Mr. L. Nelleman and issued by the owners Wu Ch'ing-an and others, is not legally valid. A joint survey should be held for the property, and the Consul is requested to contact the Land Surveying Office in Shanghai to fix a time for the survey.
= 2035 Konsulatsarkiver. Shanghai. Korrespondancesager m.v. 1911: nr. 96E.

504.

Date: (28 June 1911) - (Hsüan-t'ung 3), 6, 3.
From: Liu Yen-yi, Military Intendant, Shanghai.
To: Peter Theodor Raaschou, Consul-General of Denmark, Shanghai.
Letter stating that the Intendant wishes to express his thanks to Captain Jensen of the Danish steamer "Indien" for saving the lives of six shipwrecked Chinese fishermen.
= 2035 Konsulatsarkiver. Shanghai. Korrespondancesager m.v. 1911: nr. 102.

505.

Date: 3 July 1911 - (Hsüan-t'ung 3), 6, 8.
From: Ts'eng Mien-chi, Manager of the Land Surveying Office, Shanghai.
To: Peter Theodor Raaschou, Consul-General of Denmark, Shanghai.
Letter stating that the joint survey of the land rented by Mr. L. Nelleman will take place on the 6th at 3 o'clock.
= 2035 Konsulatsarkiver. Shanghai. Korrespondancesager m.v. 1911: nr. 96G.

506.

Date: 9 July 1911 - (Hsüan-t'ung 3), 6, 14.
From: Wu Chao-pang, Intendant of the Police in Kiangsu.
To: Peter Theodor Raaschou, Consul-General of Denmark,
    Shanghai.
Letter stating that Wu Chao-pang has been appointed
Intendant of the Police in Kiangsu and that he would like
to visit the Consulate on the 11th inst.
= 2035 Konsulatsarkiver. Shanghai. Korrespondancesager
m.v. 1911: L. nr. 4.

507.

Date: (17 July 1911) - (Hsüan-t'ung 3), 6, 22.
From: Ts'eng Mien-chi, Manager of the Land Surveying
    Office, Shanghai.
To: Peter Theodor Raaschou, Consul-General of Denmark,
    Shanghai.
Letter stating that a survey has been held for the land
rented by Mr. L. Nelleman. The deed of property has been
issued and a fee for the survey, 304 dollars, should be
paid to the Land Surveying Office.
= 2035 Konsulatsarkiver. Shanghai. Korrespondancesager
m.v. 1911: nr. 96B.

508.

Date: (7 August 1911) - (Hsüan-t'ung 3), Jun6, 13.
Invitation to visit five Chinese officials at Suchou on
the 7th of August.
= 2035 Konsulatsarkiver. Shanghai. Korrespondancesager
m.v. 1911: L. nr. 3.

509.

Date: 12 August 1911 - (Hsüan-t'ung 3), Jun6, 18.
From: Liu Yen-yi, Military Intendant, Shanghai.
To: Peter Theodor Raaschou, Consul-General of Denmark,
    Shanghai.
Letter stating that two copies of the deeds of property
for the land rented by Mr. L. Nelleman have been officially
stamped after the holding of the joint survey. They are
herewith enclosed.
= 2035 Konsulatsarkiver. Shanghai. Korrespondancesager
m.v. 1911: nr. 96C.

510.

Date: (16 August 1911) - (Hsüan-t'ung 3), Jun6, 22.
From: Ts'eng Mien-chi, Manager of the Land Surveying
    Office, Shanghai.
To: Peter Theodor Raaschou, Consul-General of Denmark,
    Shanghai.
Letter stating that four maps and one deed of property
for the land rented by Mr. L. Nelleman are hereby enclosed.
Appended: two copies of the map of the property.
= 2035 Konsulatsarkiver. Shanghai. Korrespondancesager
m.v. 1911: nr. 96F.

511.

Date: (19 August 1911) - (Hsüan-t'ung 3), Jun6, 25.
From: Liu Yen-yi, Military Intendant, Shanghai.
To: Peter Theodor Raaschou, Consul-General of Denmark,
    Shanghai.
Letter stating that a joint survey should be held for the
land bought by Mrs. Lilian Forum. The Land Surveying
Office has been instructed to this effect.
= 2035 Konsulatsarkiver. Shanghai. Korrespondancesager
m.v. 1911: nr. 121C.

512.

Date: 25 August 1911 - (Hsüan-t'ung 3), 7, 2.
From: Ts'eng Mien-chi, Manager of the Land Surveying
    Office, Shanghai.
To: Peter Theodor Raaschou, Consul-General of Denmark,
    Shanghai.
Letter stating that a joint survey of the land bought by
Mrs. Lilian Forum is to be held on the 28th August at
3 o'clock.
= 2035 Konsulatsarkiver. Shanghai. Korrespondancesager
m.v. 1911: nr. 121B.

513.

Date: (7 September 1911) - (Hsüan-t'ung 3), 7, 15.
From: Ts'eng Mien-chi, Manager of the Land Surveying
    Office, Shanghai.
To: Peter Theodor Raaschou, Consul-General of Denmark,
    Shanghai.
Letter stating that a map has been made for the land
bought by Mrs. Lilian Forum. The fee for the survey, 4
dollars, should be forwarded to the Land Surveying Office.
= 2035 Konsulatsarkiver. Shanghai. Korrespondancesager
m.v. 1911: nr. 121A.

514.

Date: *30 September 1911.*
Agreement between China and the Great Northern Telegraph Company concerning the additional cable which is to be laid on the telegraph-line between Amoy and Kulangsu.
= Store Nordiske Arkiv.

515.

Date: *(12 October 1911) - (Hsüan-t'ung 3), 8, 21.*
From: *Liu Yen-yi, Military Intendant, Shanghai.*
To: *Peter Theodor Raaschou, Consul-General of Denmark, Shanghai.*
Letter stating that the deeds of the property for the land bought by Mrs. Lilian Forum have been prepared and stamped officially. They are herewith enclosed and the Consul is requested to forward them to the owner.
Appended: Map of the property bought by Mrs. Lilian Forum.
= 2035 Konsulatsarkiver. Shanghai. Korrespondancesager m.v. 1911: nr. 121E.

516.

Date: *(23 October 1911) - (Hsüan-t'ung 3), 9, 3.*
Printed letter issued by the Managers of the Red Cross Society stating that extra equipment is needed by the staff of the Red Cross Society at the Emergency Hospital at Hank'ou, where the wounded from the recent fights between the revolutionaries and government troops are being treated by Dr. Birger Olesen and others. The Red Cross Society will arrange a meeting at Shanghai to collect money for the Hospital.
= 2035 Konsulatsarkiver. Shanghai. Korrespondancesager m.v. 1911: L. nr. 2.

517.

Date: *(November 1911) - Year 4609 after Huangti, 9, -.*
From: *The Military Government of the Republic of China.*
To: *Peter Theodor Raaschou, Consul-General of Denmark, Shanghai.*
Communication stating that after Shanghai has been conquered, the Military Government of the Republic of China has appointed officials for the important posts in the administration. The administration will co-operate with the consuls for the establishment of peace and the defence of Shanghai. A list of the officials appointed is included in the communication.
= 2035 Konsulatsarkiver. Shanghai. Korrespondancesager m.v. 1911: nr. 165E.

518.

Date: (November 1911) - Year 4609 after Huangti, 9, -.
From: Ch'en Ch'i-mei, Commander of the Military Government, Shanghai.
To: Peter Theodor Raaschou, Consul-General of Denmark, Shanghai.
Announcement stating that South-East China has been liberated from the despotic rule of the Ch'ing dynasty. A Military Government of the Republic of China has been established on the 4th of November and Ch'en Ch'i-mei has been appointed Commander at the Military Government of Shanghai. The Commander would like to express his determined will to co-operate on friendly terms with the Danish Consul-General.
= 2035 Konsulatsarkiver. Shanghai. Korrespondancesager m.v. 1911: nr. 165D.

519.

Date: (9 November 1911) - Year 4609 after Huangti, 9, 19.
From: Li Chung-yü, Superintendant of the People's Government, Shanghai.
To: T. Hansen, Consul of Denmark, Shanghai.
Communication notifying the Consul of the appointment of Li Chung-yü as Superintendant of the People's Government of Shanghai.
= 2035 Konsulatsarkiver. Shanghai. Korrespondancesager m.v. 1911: nr. 165C.

520.

Date: (9 November 1911) - Year 4609 after Huangti, 9, 19.
From: Li Chung-yü, Superintendant of the People's Government, Shanghai.
To: T. Hansen, Consul of Denmark, Shanghai.
Communication notifying the appointment of a Commissioner of the People's Government, Wu Hsiang, a Commissioner of Law, Huang Ch'ing-lan, a Commissioner of Police, Mu Hsiang-yao, and a Mayor of Shanghai, Mo Hsi-lun. Appended: a list of the new officials.
= 2035 Konsulatsarkiver. Shanghai. Korrespondancesager m.v. 1911: nr. 165B.

521.

Date: 22 November 1911 - (Year 4609 after Huangti, 10), 2.
From: Ts'ai Hsü-tung and Hsü Chi-hsiang, Commissioners of
    Foreign Affairs, Shanghai.
To: Peter Theodor Raaschou, Consul-General of Denmark,
    Shanghai.
Letter stating that on account of the appointment of
Ts'ai Hsü-tung and Hsü Chi-hsiang as Commissioners of
Foreign Affairs in Shanghai, they will visit the Consulate
on the 23rd inst.
= 2035 Konsulatsarkiver. Shanghai. Korrespondancesager
m.v. 1911: nr. 165A.

522.

Date: (1 December 1911) - Year 4609 after Huangti, 10, 11.
From: Li, Military Commander of Shanghai.
To: Peter Theodor Raaschou, Consul-General of Denmark,
    Shanghai.
Communication notifying the Consul of the appointment of
Li to the post as Military Commander of Shanghai.
= 2035 Konsulatsarkiver. Shanghai. Korrespondancesager
m.v. 1911: nr. 165F.

THE INDEXES

The following section contains two indexes to the manuscripts treated in the catalogue. The first index lists the names of Chinese officials as well as Danish Consuls etc. when they occur in the addresses of the manuscripts. The second index is a list of all the names mentioned in the summaries of each manuscript in the catalogue. At the same time the subjects treated in the manuscripts are included in the way that all the words which I have thought would give a clue to the contents of the manuscript have been listed in this index.

The numbers in the indexes refer to the number of each item in the catalogue.

Index to Names in the Addresses

Alford, E.F.
190,194,196,200,201,204.

Allum, Walter
93,178,182,189.

Bille, Steen Andersen
59,61,62,63,64,67.

Board of Trade
100,102,106,107,108,109,
110,111,112,113,116,121,
122,123,124,125,127,128,
129,130,131,132,134,136,
143,144,145,147,150,154,
163,166,171,172,173,174,
176.

Bock, Carl Alfred
217.

Chang
157,177,188.

Chang Chen
286.

Chang Ch'i-ch'uai
99.

Chang Mei-ch'üan
198.

Chang Meng-yüan
168.

Ch'en Ch'i
473,487.

Ch'en Ch'i-mei
518.

Ch'en Ming-chih
218,219,220,221,222,223,
227,229,230,231,232,233,
235,238,242,244,245,258,
259,326.

Ch'en T'ung-shu
264,266,267,268,269,276,
282.

Ch'eng-Ts'un
184.

Chin Hsüeh-hsien
257.

Ch'in
234.

Ch'i-Ying
3.

Chou
185.

Chu
186.

Chu Sung-shan
175.

Ch'ung-Hou
59.

Cruickshank, W.A.
207,208,209,210.

DeLano, M.M.
103,138,166,167,168,176.

Dircks, H.A.
142,157.

Dreyer, H.
138.

En
201.

Fang
224.

Grosse, V. de
290.

Hagberg, Filip
292,295,297,301.

Hansen, Peter
3.

Hansen, T.
445,446,447,449,450,451,
453,454,455,456,457,459,
460,465,472,519,520.

Harton
131.

He Fu-hai
285.

Henningsen
163,180.

Ho Ching
183.

Hsia
190.

Hsin Ch'in
345.

Hsü
81, 236, 238.

Hsü Chao-feng
263.

Hsü Chi-hsiang
521.

Hsüeh Huan
8,9,10.

Hsü-T'ung
187,191,194.

Hu Ch'ang-t'u
243,248.

Hu T'iao-yüan
368,369,462,468,469,482,
486.

Huang Fang
29,30,31,32,33,35,40,41,
42,43,44,45,46,47,48,49.

Imperial Chinese Telegraph
Company
211,212.

Jui-Ch'ui
283,312,313,314,315,316,
317,319,321,322,323,324,
325,326,327,328,329,330,
331,332,335,337,338,339,
340,341,346,347,348,349.

Keswick, William
41,42,43,44,45,46,47,48,
49,50,51,52,53,54,55,56,
57,58,60,65,66,68,69,70,
71,72,73,74,75,76,77,79,
80,81,82,83,84,85,86,87,
88,89,91.

Kolessoff, N.
496.

Krag-Juel-Vind-Frijs, C.E.
94,96,97,98.

Kristy, C.P.
382,392,439.

Ku
142.

Kuan Chiung
334,344,492,501.

Kuo
301.

Leigh-Smith, A.G.G.
278,279,280,283,284,285,
286,291.

Lemann, William
99,102,104.

Li
522.

Li A-wen
199.

Li Chung-yü
519,520.

Li Heng-sung
61,62,63.

Li Ho-nien
101,105,137,158,162,167.

Li Hsi-chieh
305.

Li Hung-chang
67,180,181.

Liang
208,215.

Liang Ju-hao
357,358,359,360,361,363,
370,372,373,374.

Liao
93.

Lin Ch'ing-yi
117,153.

Lin Kuei
4,5,6.

Liu
200,250.

Liu Hsün-kao
61,62,63.

Liu Yen-yi
476,479,480,481,483,485,
488,489,490,491,493,495,
502,503,504,509,511,515.

Lü Hai-huan
292,295,297,299,333.

Lu Hsin-yüan
103.

Lu Li-hsien
320.

MacGregor, John
192,193,198,199,202,203,
205,206,213,216.

MacHaffie, David
214,215.

Meyer, William
354,391,419,477.

Military Government of
the Republic of China
517.

Ministry of Foreign
Affairs
496.

Mixed Court
78.

Nieh Ch'i-kuei
206,213,217.

Nieh Tsung-hsi
394,397.

Nieh Yüan-lung
245.

O-Mi-Ta
1.

Pan Chün-chang
133.

Pao Yi
343,362,371,386,388,391,
395,396,404,412,413,419,
421,433,434,455,456,457,
459,460,461,464,465,477,
500.

Pao-Heng
165.

P'an Chün-chang
119,126.

Percival, Alexander
8,9,10.

P'eng Ao
179.

Ping Ke
281.

Popoff, N.A.
218,219,220,221,222,223,
224,225,226,227,228,229,
230,231,232,233,234,235,
236,238,239,242,243,244,
245,251,267,268,269.

Price, W.G.
105.

P'u-An
178.

Raaschou, Peter Theodor
296,298,299,300,303,304,
306,307,308,309,311,312,
313,314,315,316,317,319,
320,324,325,326,327,328,
329,330,331,332,333,334,
335,336,337,338,339,340,
341,342,343,344,345,346,
347,348,349,350,351,352,
353,355,356,357,358,359,
360,361,362,363,366,368,
369,370,371,372,373,374,
375,376,377,379,380,383,
384,385,386,388,389,394,
395,396,397,398,399,404,
405,406,407,408,410,411,
412,413,414,415,416,417,
418,420,421,423,424,425,
426,427,428,429,430,433,
434,435,438,440,441,448,
452,458,461,462,463,464,
466,467,468,469,471,473,
474,475,476,478,479,480,
481,482,483,484,485,486,
487,488,489,490,491,492,
493,494,495,500,501,502,
503,504,505,506,507,509,
510,511,512,513,515,517,
518,521,522.

Raasløff, W.R.
118,139,141.

Robertson, D.B.
4,5,6,7,

Shen Pao-chen
115.

Sheng Hsüan-huai
297,299,333,440,475.

Smith, Herbert
211,212.

Sun To-hsin
204,207,210,214.

Szu-T'u Hsü
140,146,148,155,160,161,
162.

T'an Chung-lin
226.

T'ang Pao-chien
239,242,244,245,251,258,
259.

Teng Wen-t'o
307.

Te-T'ai
196.

Tiedeman, P.H.
305.

Ting Chia-wei
120,138.

Ting Jih-ch'ang
60,65,66,68,69,70,71,72,
73,74,75,76,77,79,80.

T'ieh
189,200.

Tsai
216.

Ts'ai Hsü-tung
521.

Ts'ai Nai-huang
377,379,380,381,383,384,
385,389,398,399,405,407,
408,410,411,414,416,417,
418,420,423,424,425,426,
427,428,429,430,435,438,
441,445,446,447,448,449,
450,451,452,453,454,458,
463,466,467,471,472,474,
478.

Ts'eng Mien-chi
505,507,510,512,513.

Tseng Yün
406.

Tsungli Yamen
64,94,96,97,98,118,139,
141.

Tun Ch'ang-tsai
241.

Waeber, L.
181.

Wang
78,82,83.

Wang Chia-t'ang
484,494.

Wang Hsieh
350,351,352,353,354,355,
356,415.

Wang K'ai-t'ai
137.

Wen-Yü
101,137,159.

Whittall, Edward
92,94.

Whittall, James
11,12,13,14,15,16,17,18,
19,20,21,22,23,24,25,26,
27,28,29,30,31,32,33,34,
35,40.

Wu Chao-pang
506.

Wu Hsü
7,11,12,13,14,15,16,17,
18,19,20,21,22,23,24,25,
26,27,28,34.

Wu T'ing-fang
292,295.

Yang Shih-ao
201,207,210,214.

Yang Wen-ting
225,228,256,258,259,276,
282.

Yang Yung-pin
1.

Yeh Yung-yüan
182.

Ying Pao-shih
50,52,53,54,55,56,57,58,
84,85,86,87,88,89,91,92,
95.

Young, W.S.
100,107,110,112,115,116,
117,119,120,122,123,124,
126,130,135,140,144,146,
147,148,150,153,154,155,
156,158,159,160,162,164,
169,170,171,172,173,174.

Yü Chao-fan
336,342.

Yüan Shu-hsün
278,279,280,284,291,296,
298,300,303,304,306,308,
309,311.

Index to Subjects and Names in Summaries

A Mao
80.

Aaberg
249,260,261.

Abrogated law
233.

Absent from office
12,18,47,52,65,69,75,77,
79,85,326,329,330,335,339,
341,346,352,373,379,383,
398,407,411,416,424,428,
445,447,448,451,488,493.

Additional cable
275,287,514.

Additional telegraph-line
in Fukien
183.

Agreement
108,151,172,173,174,180,
181,240,246,254,262,271,
272,273,274,275,302,496,
497,514.

Ahlefeldt
476.

Air-guns
323,338,340,426.

Aistrup, Adolf
309.

Alford, E.F.
207,208,209.

Allied Powers
270.

Allum, Walter
93.

American business-firm,
"Pao-lung"
32.

American mission
193.

American missionary
356.

Amoy
247.

Andersen, Meyer and Co.
312,316,325,338,349,351,
355,359,360,432,434,487,
491,498,500.

Anhui
319,470.

Anhui Railway Lottery
378.

Anti-foreign placard
110.

An-chi district
230.

Apology
304.

Appointment
10,11,14,15,16,17,19,20,
21,22,24,25,27,29,31,33,
35,45,46,50,51,54,57,58,
68,73,88,91,99,104,120,
139,140,141,168,178,184,
186,187,188,189,190,194,
200,201,204,206,207,208,
209,210,213,214,215,217,
223,230,232,234,235,236,
239,242,243,245,256,257,
259,263,264,266,267,268,
298,328,333,343,345,350,
357,361,363,376,377,394,
397,406,415,450,454,462,
479,480,482,483,484,501,
506,517,518,519,520,521,
522.

Asiatisk Kompagni
2.

Baron Haxthausen
317.

Bayonet
311.

Belgian Consul
471.

Berner, J.
296.

Bidoulac, A.
320.

Bille, Steen Andersen
59,60,61,62,63.

Birthday of the Danish
King.
321,440,441,502.

Birthday of the Empress
Dowager
334,414.

Birthday of the Kuang-hsü
Emperor
405.

Black Vicuna cloth
498.

Blockade of the port of
Fuchou
226.

Bock, Carl Alfred
217.

Bojesen, C.C.
112,145,211,212.

Boxers
270.

Boxer-rebellion
272.

Brandt, Max von
205.

Bremen
20,25,54.

British business firm
"Yi-ho"
185,191.

British Consul
191.

British Consulate
6.

British defendants
83.

British subject
269.

Brown, John McLeavy
97.

Burlinghame, A.
94,96,98.

Cables on the coast of
China
262.

Cable-houses
315.

Canton
1,2,3,14,23,237.

Caps of messenger-runners
238.

Captain Jensen
504.

Cargo
226.

Cash-book
344.

Cattle
312.

Champs, de
97.

Chang Chen
286.

Chang Jen-chün
454.

Chang Mao-chang
401.

Chang Mei-ch'üan
198.

Chang Meng-yüan
168.

Chang Yi-hsin
185.

Chang Yüan-hsing
280.

Chao
99.

Cha-p'u
370,372.

Ch'ao-chou (Swatow)
190,200,210.

Cheefoo
249,260,281.

Chekiang
370,470.

Chen Pao-yung
432.

Cheng Hsü-po
431.

Cheng Kan-t'ing
431,433.

Cheng Szu-chien
154.

"Chen-ch'ang-lung",
Chinese business firm
401,402.

Ch'en Ch'i-mei
518.

Ch'en Kuei-hsien
482.

Ch'en Ming-chih
223,227,242.

Ch'en Ts'eng-p'ei
298.

Ch'en T'ung-shu
264,266,267,268.

Ch'en Yü
443.

Ch'en Yü-ch'ing
443,457,460,465.

Ch'eng-Ts'un
184.

Chi Chi
412.

Chiang-pu district
250,254,255.

Chihli
265,381,449.

Chih-Kang
96,98.

Chin Hsüeh-hsien
257.

China
297,299.

Chinchiang
301,348.

Chinese business firm,
"Chen-ch'ang-lung"
401,402.

Chinese business firm,
"Chih-hsing-ch'ang-chi"
456,459.

Chinese business firm,
"Fu-ch'an"
401,402.

Chinese business firm,
"Heng-sheng"
386,393.

Chinese business firm,
"Hsiang-yüan"
307.

Chinese business firm,
"Hung-hsing"
116.

Chinese business firm,
"Mou-ch'ang"
477,492.

Chinese business firm,
"Pao-hung"
386,387,395,413.

Chinese emigrants
8.

Chinese emigration
101,102.

Chinese Emperor
37,67.

Chinese government
180.

Chinese islands
262.

Chinese law
8.

Chinese merchants
employed by foreign
firms
155.

Chinese Military
Authorities
325.

Chinese Ministry of
Foreign Affairs
327,328.

Chinese mission to the
Western nations
94,96,97,98.

Chinese New Year
84.

Chinese notice
334.

Chinese officials at
Fuchou
114.

Chinese officials at
Shanghai
364,390.

Chinese officials at
Suchou
508.

Chinese plaintiffs
82,83.

Chinese police
290.

Chinese Red Cross
Society
475.

Chinese settlement
464.

Chinese soldiers
123,125,370,372.

Chinese subject
269.

Chin-chiang
170.

Ch'in
234.

Chou
103.

Chou Ching-fang
483.

Chou Hsing-yi
164.

Christophersen
283.

Chu
230.

Chu Sung-shan
175.

Churches
130.

Chusan Islands
43.

Ch'ung-ming district
280.

Commercial Pacific Cable Company
302.

Common people
231.

Communications, official
147.

Competition
262.

Comprador
185,320.

Condolences
365,367.

Confiscation
360.

Consulate
202,233,358.

Consulates in China
3.

Contraband ammunition
32.

Contract
348.

Contract of employment
212.

Correspondence between Danish Ambassador and Chinese Authorities
67.

Count Ahlefeldt
476.

Craig, Robert
188.

Cruickshank, W.A.
207,208,209.

Cunningham, Edward
48.

Customs drawbacks
72.

Customs-house
339.

Damage on telegraph-cable
280,284.

Danes, attacked by Chinese
123,125,143,146.

Danes, trade at Canton
3.

Danish business firm, "Hsin-t'ai-ch'ang"
301.

Danish business firm, "Wang-fu"
80,81.

Danish captain
248.

Danish Consul
367.

Danish Consulate
147,327,328.

Danish Consul-General to Manila
4,5,6.

Danish Envoy
3,59,60,61,62,63,115,142, 158,159,160,161,162.

Danish firm Andersen, Meyer and Co.
312,316,325,338,349,351, 355,359,360,432,434,487, 491,498,500.

Danish firm Hillebrandt and Co.
477,492.

Danish firm H. Wessel
418.

Danish firm Schiller and Co.
472.

Danish business firm W. Funder and Co.
431,433,443,444,455,457, 460,465.

Danish firms
468,473.

Danish King
63,299,321,440,441,502.

Danish lawyer
320.

Danish Legation at Peking
292,476.

Danish missionaries
358,385,389,463,490.

Danish nationality
42.

Danish ship
30.

Danish steamer "Indien"
504.

Danish subjects
467.

Death of the Empress Dowager Tz'u-hsi
365,419,420,421.

Death of the Governor of Fukien
160.

Death of the Kuang-hsü Emperor
366,420.

Death of the wife of the uncle of Tuan-Fang
367,409.

Debt
320.

Deeds of property
107,117,134,150,248,278, 306,507,509,510,515.

Delivery of foreign goods
203.

Delivery of goods
307,386.

Demobilization of soldiers
277.

Denmark
19,41,91,93,98,186,187,
188,211,213,217,277,295,
297,299,324.

Designation of an office
238.

Deutch Niederlandishe
Telegraphie Gesellshaft
302.

Disturbances
121,123,124,137,156.

Dog-hunting
332.

Dreyer
112.

Duty
313.

Duty tariffs
3.

East Asiatic Company
291,456,459,485.

Eastern Extension Telegraph-
Company
240,247,302,496,497.

Edict, Imperial
1,95,96,97,98.

Embezzlement
309.

Emergency hospital
516.

Emigrants, Chinese
8.

Emigration
101,102,288,289.

Emigration Act of 1866
89,90.

Emperor of China
63.

Empress Dowager Tz'u-hsi,
birthday of
354,414.

Empress Dowager Tz'u-hsi,
death of
366,419,420,421.

En
201.

English business firm
395.

English officer
319.

Escort by Chinese
soldiers
126,127,128,129.

Establishment of a
telegraph-school
173,174.

Exchange of ratified
treaties
59,60,61,62,63.

Expenditures for repairs
on the telegraph-line
163,166,167.

Export
312,314,426.

E.S. Petersen and Co.
334,336,344,362,371.

Fan Tseng-hsiang
449,450,454.

Fang-k'ou
124,125,126,127,128,133,
134,143,145,146.

Fa-hua village
332.

Fengshui
183.

Fight between revolutionaries and government troops
516.

Fight with Japanese ships
228.

Fishing-rods obstruction to the passage of ships
177.

Fitz-Roy, G.H.
30,87.

Flour
370,372.

Forbes, J.B.
48,68.

Foreign business firm
348.

Foreign business firm, "He-p'ing"
342.

Foreign firms
238,258.

Foreign governments
221.

Foreign settlement of Shanghai
71.

Foreign ships
319.

Foreign steamers
244.

Foreign warships surveying the coast of China
176.

Foreigners, protection
221,231.

Foreigners travelling along the coast of China
244.

Foreigners travelling in the interior of China
175.

Forms for Registration
467.

Forts, at Shanghai
192, 228.

Fortuny, Eusebio de
23,55.

Forum, Lilian
511,512,513,515.

France
14,31,43,56,73,88.

Fraud
334.

French merchant
458.

French Mixed Court
298.

Fuchou
115,126,127,128,144,152,
153,165,173,223,226,227,
264,266.

Fuchou officials
114.

Funeral for the Kuang-hsü Emperor
438.

"Fu-ch'an", Chinese business firm
401,402.

"Fu-ch'ang", Russian business firm
179,224.

"Fu-shun", a Chinese ship
280,284.

Gambling
471.

German Ambassador
205.

German business firm
464.

German Legation at Peking
485.

Germany
279,316.

Goertz, H.
422.

Gram, Thomas D.
301.

Graveyard
117,134,154.

Great Britain
15,24,33,35,51,83,225,269.

Great Northern Telegraph Company
100,103,105,106,107,108,
109,117,121,122,123,125,
127,128,129,131,132,133,
134,137,138,143,144,146,
150,151,152,153,154,163,
164,165,166,167,169,170,
171,172,173,180,181,183,
198,246,247,262,271,272,
273,274,275,282,284,285,

Great Northern Telegraph Company (continued)
287,289,290,300,302,303,
304,305,315,322,382,392,
469,496,497,514.

Guards at the German Legation at Peking
485.

Guns
1,322,360.

Hagberg, Filip
292,295,297.

Hamburg
16,20,25,34,54.

Hangchou
372.

Hank'ou
310,314,340,516.

Hannover
17.

Hansen, Peter
3.

Hansen, Thomas
32.

Hart, Robert
87.

Haxthausen
317.

Hearson and Co.
255.

Heinsen, R.
20,25,54.

Helland
169.

"Heng-sheng", Chinese business firm
386,393.

Henningsen
111,144,153,166,167,181.

"He-p'ing", foreign business firm
342.

Hillebrandt and Co.
372,386,387,388,393,395,
396,401,402,404,412,413,
477,492.

Hippisley
295.

Ho
223,230.

Hogg, William
16.

Holland
279.

Holst, J.M.
198,199.

Honan
470.

Hoskier
112.

Hsi Fu-shun
284.

Hsi Yen-yü
284.

Hsia
190,436.

"Hsiang-yüan", Chinese business firm
307.

Hsiao T'ien
185.

Hsieh Chin-jung
344,362,371.

Hsieh Ju-chou
250,254.

Hsieh Ping-liang
250.

Hsin Ch'in
345.

"Hsin-t'ai-ch'ang", Danish business firm
301.

Hsü
236.

Hsü Chao-feng
263.

Hsü Chi-hsiang
521.

Hsüan-t'ung Emperor
423,427.

Hsüeh Huan
22.

Hsü-T'ung
194.

Hu Ch'ang-t'u
243.

Huang Ch'ing-lan
520.

Huang Fang
29,44,46,47,49,50.

Huang Jui-ch'ui
144.

Huang Ku-sun
283.

Huang Mao-chi
388,396,404.

Huang Tsan-ch'ao
381.

"Huang-ch'i"-Company
2.

Hughes
192.

"Hung-Hsing", Chinese
business firm
116.

Hunting
319,332.

H. Wessel, Danish
business firm
418.

Illegal anchoring
30.

Illegal Opium-shop
241.

Illness
43.

Immoral singing and
misbehaving
303.

Imperial Chinese Telegraph
Company
211.

Imperial Edict
94,96,97,276,496.

Imperial Maritime Customs
30,87,403.

Import
313,314,316,317,322,323,
325,338,340,349,351,355,
359,360,418,472,485,491.

Indemnity
138.

"Indien", Danish steamer
504.

Insanity
211,212.

International Settle-
ment in Shanghai
471.

Japan
324,458.

Japanese ships
218,228.

Japanese spies
231.

Japanese students
466.

Jensen, Captain
504.

Joint purse
240,256,302.

Joint survey
285,503,505,507,509,511,
512.

Judgement
465.

Jui-Ch'ui
326,329,330,331,337,339,
341,346,347,350,355,375.

Jung Chi
444,455.

Keswick, William
41,91.

Kiangnan
22.

Kiangsi
470.

Kiangsu
11,22,250,254,255,470,
484,506.

Kierulff
195,197.

Kirchof, Hakon J.H.
252,253,254.

Kofoed
175.

Kristiansen, N.
318,490.

Krogh, Constant Alexander
308.

Ku Po-hua
462.

Ku Yang-ch'ing
303.

Kuan Chiung
334,501.

Kuangtung province
196.

Kuang-hsü Emperor,
birthday of the
405.

Kuang-hsü Emperor,
death of the
366,420,421.

Kuang-hsü Emperor,
funeral of the
438.

Kung Chao-yüan
192,206.

K'un-shan
18.

Kweichow
466.

Lack of evidence
392.

Land Surveying Office
296,298,300,363,381,462,
482,483,507,511,513.

Land tax
368,369,468,486.

Lao Wang
442.

Law, Chinese
8.

Law abrogated
233.

Laws for Registration of
National Subjects
437,474.

Lawsuit.
216.

Lawsuit against a Chinese
subject
280,282,283,284,288,289,
290,303,304,305,307,334,
336,344,362,370,372,382,
386,387,388,391,392,393,
395,396,401,402,404,412,
413,431,433,434,439,442,
443,444,455,456,457,459,
460,465,477,478,498,500.

Lawsuit against a
foreigner
80,202,281,320,332,336,
356,422.

Lawsuits between foreign
and Chinese subjects
461.

Lawyer, Danish
320.

Lease
278,300.

Lease of a garden
248.

Lease of a property
179.

Legal possession
154.

Legal settlement
179.

Letters, unofficial
148.

Li
522.

Li A-wen
199.

Li Ch'ang-chün
483.

Li Chi-fu
422.

Li Chung-yü
519.

Li Heng-sung
59,63.

Li Ho-nien
158,162.

Li Hsing-tung
402.

Li Hsi-chieh
261.

Li Hung-chang
62,197.

Li Liang-ch'en
391.

Li Shu-t'ang
336.

Liang Hsien-ch'en
412.

Liang Ju-hao
357,361,373,374.

Liaoning
318.

Likin-tax
193.

Lin Ken-hsien
391.

Lin Kuei
4,5.

Lin Tsun-po
144.

Lindberg, C.E.
265.

Lindholm
278.

Liu
195,197,200.

Liu Hsün-kao
59,63.

Liu Yen-yi
479,480,488,489,493,495,
501.

Liu Yi-yün
462,482.

Loan to China
497.

Local officials
105,123,124,288.

147

Local population
466.

Lu Hsin-yüan
103,104.

Lu Li-hsien
320.

Lu Tzu-tung
216.

Lü Hai-huan
279,297,333.

Lübeck
34

Lübeck and Bremen
54.

"Lyeemoon"
237.

Macao
101.

MacGregor, John
213.

MacHaffie, David
214,215.

Machinery
348.

Magistrate's Office
9.

Magnussen, Svend Aage
470.

Manilla, Danish Consul-General to
4,5,6.

Markham, J.
35.

Mauboussin, M.V.
31,43.

Ma-lu
356.

Meadows, T.T.
15,24.

Medhurst
24.

Meeting on Prohibition of Opium Smoking
430.

Merchant ships
222,226,228.

Merchants
229.

Messenger-runners
238,290.

Miao-chiang
466.

Military Authorities in China
317.

Military examinations
158,160,162.

Military Government
517.

Military Government of the Republic of China
518.

Min river, piracy on
258.

Mined entrance to the port of Fuchou
219,220,222,226.

Mining battalion
219.

Ministry of Foreign
Affairs
276.

Ministry of Foreign Affairs
in China
292,295.

Ministry of Post and
Communication
496.

Min-yü-jih-pao
458.

Missionaries
130,193,205,358.

Missionary, American
356.

Missionary, Danish
318,385,389,463,490.

Missionary, Russian
119.

Mixed Court
203,388,419,434,442,443,
444,461.

Mo Hsi-lun
520.

Money-collecting
516.

Money-orders
251.

Monopoly on construction
of telegraphs in China
180.

Montiguy, C. de
14.

Moore, John
45.

"Mou-ch'ang", Chinese
business firm
477,492.

Mu Hsiang-yao
520.

Mukden
308.

Munoz, Domingo
23.

Munthe-Brun, Johan
310.

Møller, C.
478.

M.L. Kristensen and Co.
311.

Nanking
324,388,396,454.

Nanyang Industrial
Exhibition
473,487.

Nan-ta road
264.

Nan-t'ai
184,247.

Naval attaché
265.

Negotiations
7,109,292,295,496.

Nellemann, L.
306,499,503,505,507,509,
510.

New Agreement on the
telegraph-line
108.

New negotiations on the
telegraph-line
109.

New Regulations for the Customs
7.

New Year Greetings
44,74,95,364.

Nieh Ch'i-kuei
206.

Nieh Tsung-hsi
394,397.

Nieh Yüan-lung
235,245.

Ningchou
283.

Ningpo
223,336.

Ningpo road
434.

North China Coal Company
422.

Notebooks
116.

Notice to Mariners
245.

Obituary
409,436.

Office of Foreign Affairs in Fuchou
264,266.

Officer, English
319.

Official communications
147.

Official telegrams
180.

Officials
229.

Oldenburg
17,28.

Olesen, Birger
516.

Opium
92.

Opium-shop, illegal
241.

Pagoda-line
151,152.

Pai-tiao-ling
250,254.

Pao-Yi
343,362,371,455,456,492.

Pao-ch'eng Coal Mining Company
250,252,253,254,255.

"Pao-hung", Chinese business firm
386,387,395,413.

"Pao-lung", American business firm
32.

Pao-shan district
278,303,304,315,369,463, 467,468,469,482,486.

Parkes, H.J.
51.

Passport
100,111,112,113,119,196, 205,249,260,261,308,310, 318,385,389,432,470,490.

P'an Chün-chang
104,140,160.

P'an Kuang-ch'ü
109,110.

150

Peace Protocol of 1901
276,292.

Peiyang Naval Department
265.

Peking
195,205,270,272,273,287,
292,295,310,448,476,485.

People's Government of
Shanghai
519.

Personnel at the Consulate
327,328.

Petition
175,180,198,241,281,320,
336,387,393,401,402,422,
431,442,443,444.

Petitions to the Mixed
Court
461.

Pien Shih-ch'üan
232.

Piloting
219,220,222.

Ping Ke
281.

Piracy on the Min river
258.

Pistols
317,491.

P'ing-t'an Island
288,289,293,294.

Plain language in
telegrams
229.

Plundering of telegraph-
line
108.

Police, Chinese
290.

Popoff, N.A.
218.

Port Clearance
72.

Portugal
57.

Portuguese Emperor
101.

Poulsen
303,304.

Practice with guns
192.

Prince Valdemar
324.

Probst, W.
17,28.

Proclamation
157,167,270,293,294,471.

Proclamation by the
British Governor of
Hongkong
64.

Promissory notes
116.

Protection of Danish ships
64.

Protection of foreigners
119,221,244,322,491.

Protection of Taiwan
136.

Protection of telegraph-
equipment
126,127,128,129,131,132,
133,134.

Protection of telegraph-line
106,118,122,134,142.

Prussia
58.

Prussian warships
64.

Public house
290.

Purchase of the telegraph-
line between Fuchou and
Amoy
138,169,171,172.

P'u-An
178.

Raaschou, Peter Theodor
438,487.

Raasløff, Waldemar Rudolf
116,142,158,159,160,161,
162.

Rablez, M.B. de
88.

Rameau, G.C.
43.

Ratified Tariff Agreement
297,299.

Red Cross Society
475,516.

Regulations for elimination
of gambling-houses
71.

Regulations for Importation
of Arms and Ammunition
349,360,400,403,418,472,
476.

Regulations for telegrams
in secret language
225.

Removal of the telegraph-
line
164.

Rent of houses
434.

Rental of a house
281.

Residence of the Governor
of Kiangsu
61,62.

Resistance of the common
people
105,125,165,183.

Returned to office
13,49,53,66,70,76,86,
182,331,337,341,347,353,
374,375,380,384,399,408,
410,417,425,429,435,446,
453,489,495.

Revolvers
485.

Rice
291.

Rifles
311,314,316,349,351,355,
476.

Robbery, by Chinese
subjects
144,153.

Robbery, by foreigners
78,82,83.

Robertson, D.B.
15.

Rock
237.

Rodriguez, W.A.
45.

Rules for Registration of
National Subjects
474.

Russia
21,241,432.

Russian Ambassador at
Peking
295.

Russian business firm,
"Fu-ch'ang"
179,224.

Russian business firm,
"Shun-feng"
224.

Russian missionary
119.

Samples
351,355.

Schiller and Co.
472.

Schultz
115,135,136.

Schwensen
382,392,439.

Secret language in
telegrams
225,229,233.

Security for contracts
203.

Sedanchair-bearers
153.

"Sen-t'ai"-shop
443,455,460.

Seward
27.

Shanghai
4,19,29,40,46,59,60,61,
255,271,274,275,277,291,
292,298,320,332,350,361,
364,381,390,394,396,397,
458,463,479,483,499,503,
516,517,518,521,522.

Shanghai officials
74,84,321.

Shantung
249,260,261.

Shen Pao-chen
136.

Shen Yüan-fu
464.

Sheng Hsüan-huai
277,297,333,440,475.

"Shen-chou" newspaper
452.

Ships and crews
258.

Shipwrecked Chinese
fishermen
504.

Shooting Chinese subjects
319,332.

Shop in Peking
195.

"Shun-feng", Chinese
business firm
498,500.

"Shun-feng", Russian
business firm
224.

"Sigh of the People"-
daily
458.

Singapore
216.

Sino-Japanese war
218,219,221,222.

Smith
27.

Soldiers, Chinese
123,125,370,372.

South Manchuria
358.

Spain
23,45,55,88.

Spelter
325.

Spies, Japanese
231.

Sporting guns
418,472.

Steamers, foreign
244.

Stephen
80,81.

Su Ching
290.

Suchou
375,500.

Sun Chia-ku
96,98.

Sun Fu-hsiang
348.

Sun To-hsin
204,210.

Sungchiang
394,397.

Supply of machinery
348.

Swatow (Ch'ao-chou)
190,200,210.

Sweden and Norway
40,48,68.

Swindling
431.

Szu-T'u Hsü
140,161.

Taiwan, protection of
136.

Taku
271,272,273,274,275,287.

Tariff Agreement
292,295,297,299.

Tariff Regulations
36.

Tax, extra
1.

Tax, land
224,356,368,369.

Taylor
295.

T'ai-p'ing rebels
42.

T'an Chung-lin
232.

T'ang Feng-kang
382,392,439.

T'ang He-lou
387,413.

T'ang Pao-chien
239,242,256.

T'ang Shao-k'ang
478.

Tea-business
283.

Telegrams
240.

Telegrams in plain language
229.

Telegrams in secret language
225,229,233.

Telegraph revenue
496.

Telegraph-cable
280.

Telegraph-equipment, protection of
126,127,128,129,131,132,
133,134,144,145,282.

Telegraph-line between Amoy and Kulangsu
514.

Telegraph-line between Chefoo and Taku
275.

Telegraph-line between Fuchou and Amoy
103,105,106,108,109,110,
118,121,122,125,137,138,
156,163,165,169,170,171,
172.

Telegraph-line between Nant'ai and Mawei
151,152.

Telegraph-line between Shanghai and Taku
271,274,275.

Telegraph-line between Taku, Peking, and Kiackta
273,287.

Telegraph-line between Taku and Peking
272.

Telegraph-lines in connection with Nant'ai and Amoy
247.

Telegraph-school at Fuchou
173,174.

Theft
153,305,344,382,392,433,
439.

Theft and swindling
431.

Theft of telegraph-equipment
157,282,288,289,293,294.

Thomsen
305.

Tientsin
59,195,197,359,483.

Ting Chia-wei
120,135,137,168.

Ting Jih-ch'ang
61,65,66,69,75,76,77,79.

Title of the Danish Sovereign
67.

T'ieh
189.

T'ien Chih-hsüan
177.

Toy guns
359.

Toy rifle
316.

Translation of an English
visiting card
26.

Trans-ship to harbour
226.

Treaty between Denmark
and China
30,36,37,38,39,59,64,67,
110,124,126.

Treaty between Russia and
China
21.

Ts'ai Hsü-tung
521.

Ts'ai Nai-huang
376,377,379,380,383,384,
398,399,407,408,410,411,
416,417,424,425,426,428,
429,435,441,445,446,447,
451,453,479.

Ts'ao Chi-an
464.

Tseng Yün
406.

Ts'eng-Ch'i
259.

Tsungli Yamen
96,98,134,137,148,155,
205,221,229.

Tu Chin-yung
303.

Tuan-Chin
409.

Tuan-Fang
324,348,367,409,430,438,
448,449.

Tun Ch'ang-tsai
241.

T'ung-chou
339,341.

Tz'u-hsi
365,366,419.

United States of America
10,27.

Unofficial letters
148.

Valdemar, Danish Prince
324.

Village constable
191.

Visit
158,159,160,161,162.

Visit to the British
Consulate
6.

Visit to the Consulate
44,279.

Visit to the Danish
Consulate
74,95,286,343,361,362,375,
377,413,415,440,441,480,
481,494,501,502,506,521.

Visit to the office of
the Intendant
84.

Visiting cards
390.

Vladivostock
312.

Wade, Thomas
59.

Wan Chung-an
436.

Wang Chung-yüan
436.

Wang Chia-t'ang
484.

Wang Hsieh
350,352,353,354,357,415.

Wang Hsing-ch'ing
495.

"Wang-fu", Danish business firm
80,81.

War between Denmark and Germany
62.

Warships, foreign
176.

Watchhouse
123.

Water-damaged opium, duty-free
92.

Water-works Company of Chinciang
348.

Wei
283.

Wei Ch'in-hou
251.

Wen-Yü
159.

Whampoo Water-conservacy
315.

Wheat flour
342.

Whittall, Edward
91.

Whittall, James
19,41.

Wied, Augusta
385,389.

Winter solstice
9.

Wolff, Ferdinand
4,5,6.

Woosung
285,296.

Woosung Commercial Settlement
285.

Wu Chao-pang
506.

Wu Ch'ing-an
499,503.

Wu Hsiang
520.

Wu Hsü
11,12,13,18,21,22,29.

Wu Shan-miao
216.

Wu Wen-chin
269.

Wu Yüan
363.

Wu Yüan-chi
381.

W. Funder and Co.
431,433,442,443,444,455,
457,460,465.

Yang Chia-t'ang
500.

Yang Huan-jo
307.

Yang Shih-ao
201,204,210.

Yang Wen-ting
256,268.

Yangtze river
319.

Yao-t'ung
466.

Yeh Yung-yüan
182.

Ying Pao-shih
46,50,51,52,53,85,86,95.

"Yi-ho", British business firm
185,191.

Young, W.S.
139,141.

Yü Tu
298.

Yü-Lu
265.

For Product Safety Concerns and Information please contact our EU
representative GPSR@taylorandfrancis.com
Taylor & Francis Verlag GmbH, Kaufingerstraße 24, 80331 München, Germany

www.ingramcontent.com/pod-product-compliance
Lightning Source LLC
Chambersburg PA
CBHW061838300426

44115CB00013B/2436